# JESUS
## Man for Today

# JESUS
## Man for Today

## T. RALPH MORTON

Nashville      ⊕Abingdon Press      New York

To Jenny with love

# Preface

The theme of this book has been in my mind for a long time. But when I came to write it, it took quite a different line from that which I had first planned. I had thought that we could go back and find a new understanding and a fuller meaning in the names that men in the past had given to Jesus, such as "Lord," "Redeemer," "Savior," "King," and "Son of God." But the more one thought about them, the more unsatisfactory and even misleading they seemed for men today. Words change their meanings with the years. Specific names and titles, far from growing in significance, become technical and limited in their reference. Every title newly given to Jesus in the past illuminated something fresh in men's experience of him. But, in the end, each old title diminishes our picture of Jesus and prevents us from seeing him for ourselves. It dates him and makes us think of him, not as belonging to our own day, but as belonging to the past. If we are to see him at all we have to see him in relation to our own world: we have to describe him in our own words. Jesus' question to his first disciples, after they had given him other men's answers, was: "But whom do you say that I am?" The question is still put to us. We do not answer it by quoting other men's answers, however orthodox they may claim to be.

I have been encouraged in my task by many people. I must particularly mention two: John Casteel for pushing me on and David Cairns for trying to hold me back. To the former I am specially grateful, not only for his encouragement and for the help which so much of what he writes in public and in private gives to me, but also for his kindness in introducing me to the Abingdon Press.

My debt to others is obvious. I should like particularly to thank John Wren-Lewis for permission to quote from a review of his in *The Guardian* and for all that he has contributed to my thinking by his writing and his conversation; and also to thank John McIntyre for permission to quote from his inaugural lecture as Principal of New College in the University of Edinburgh.

To Beryl Jardine who miraculously found time to type most of the book and to Carol Morton who equally miraculously did the rest I would say "Thank you."

T. R. M.

# Contents

# What Name Do We Give Him Now?

Everything is being questioned today. We ask questions, sometimes violently, about our way of life. We ask questions about the organization of our political life, about our local life, about the kind of people we want as neighbors. We ask questions about our national life: Have we sufficient say in its administration? About our international life: What responsibility have we for people of other races and nations? Should we be striving for a new kind of national life which would fit into a new kind of world order? What about our relations with our neighbors near and far? Do we want a multiracial nation? Can we see farther than a multinational world? Can we foresee a world in which divisions of race and politics and class would disappear and all men be treated

equally? What do we mean by civil rights? What is liberty
—and responsibility?

And what about God? There are plenty of questions about
God, if there is a God.

It seems as though nothing can be taken for granted any
more. For some of us such questions are more than disturb-
ing—they are menacing. They challenge the basis of all that
we have assumed as unchanging. And for most of us there is
something which we do not want to have questioned at all
because such a challenge would undermine our sense of security, and without some basic security we know that we
would never do anything at all. But such questioning is inevitable, especially when so much in our way of living and
thinking is undergoing change. We are bound to ask questions about the way that life is developing and about what
we should be doing. No one can avoid such questions. For
Christians they are quite inescapable. In asking questions
about the nature of contemporary life and of our duty to
the future we are not challenging the faith. Far from it. We
are asserting the eternal nature of the faith and acknowledg-
ing the inadequacy of all our attempts, past and present, to
express it fully in our life and thought. We should not be
surprised to be called by events to think in a different way
about ourselves, about our human situation, and about our
understanding of God from the way our forefathers and even
our fathers thought. We should be surprised if we did not.
The Christian faith is basically a call to change.

In the last decade or two the religious debate has been
focused very much on the questions of God. Where is God?
Can we any longer talk about a God "up there" now that

men have got up there? How should we now describe God? Can we still speak of him in personal terms? Can we speak of him at all? Is there a God? These questions are asked everywhere, outside the church and inside.

Strangely, the question of Jesus never seems to come up. Fifty years ago men questioned whether Jesus had ever really existed. Or, if he did, could we really know definitely anything about him? No one at that time was particularly interested in discussing God. Are men today being more daring or more profound? Are they now at last getting to the root of the matter, or are they today missing the real question—and doing so almost deliberately? For our terrifying and inescapable questions are about ourselves, about the situation we are in, about our hopes and our destiny, about the nature of human personality. These questions are not academic. They are practical. In our actions each day we are attempting to answer them. These questions are the spring behind much of student protest and political demonstration. It is safer to have an academic discussion about God. The question that really worries people is not "Where is God?" but "What is man?" and "Where is he going?" And perhaps it is safer to have an academic discussion about God than to face these questions. Among all the conflicting facets of human experience, Jesus is there—a fact to be recognized; part of the human question. The primary question is about Jesus, not about God. This is always true for the Christian, for his faith starts from Jesus. It is true also, if in a different way, for other men, for their questions are about man and nothing human is alien to that discussion.

But one would have thought that the question would have

come up: "Is Jesus relevant at all to the discussion of man today?" Can a young Jew who lived nearly two thousand years ago in a small subject nation and was put to death as a political criminal have anything to say to us in the world today? Can his short life not be seen to be repeated in the life and death of many other young men in the modern world? Why should he have any unique and universal significance? And if what he did and said had unique qualities, has it any meaning in an utterly different world now? What has he possibly to do with our new world of nuclear science, dependent economies, and mixed societies? What can he mean to the Chinese—a fifth of the world's population—or to the starving inhabitants of South America? Or, for that matter, to the affluent, sophisticated inhabitants of North America, Western Europe, and Russia? Or, if he could mean something, does he need to be freed of all the disguising wrappings of medieval thought and prescientific experience? As Teilhard de Chardin asks: "Is the Christ of the Gospels, imagined and loved within the dimensions of a Mediterranean world, capable of still embracing and still forming the centre of our prodigiously expanded universe?" [1] Is Jesus relevant at all? And, if he is, how do men see him as relevant?

The strange thing is that so many men today do see him as supremely relevant. Among the uncertainties about God, about man, and about the future, Jesus seems to remain, if not unquestioned, at least unquestionably there and raising questions for men.

Many instances could be given of the hold Jesus has on the imaginations of men today. Two must suffice.

[1] Teilhard de Chardin, *The Divine Milieu* (New York: Harper, 1960), p. 14.

## What Name Do We Give Him Now?

In the magazine *Encounter* for December, 1968, there appeared two articles by distinguished European writers. Both had been Communists. Both had expressed their disillusionment with communism by contributing to the book *The God that Failed*. In the articles in *Encounter* they were concerned, each in his own way, with Jesus. One of the writers was Arthur Koestler. He contributed an article called *Episode*.[2] The episode is the death of Jesus on the cross. It is a soliloquy by Jesus as he is taken to Calvary and nailed to the cross. It is based on the record of the Gospels and is expressed in the words of the Gospels. It is bitter and compassionate—a cry of despair against the cruelty of God; Koestler seems to find in Jesus the supreme example of human suffering, endurance, and love. He might be said to be repeating Pilate's words: "Behold the Man"—Jesus, the supreme representative of suffering humanity.

The other writer is Ignazio Silone of Italy. In an article called "What Remains: A Word about Socialism and Christianity," he discusses the attitude of a man who has been a member of the church and also of the Party, who has come out of each and yet has not abandoned the faith he held in both. Yet he can never feel part of the institution of the church or of the Party again. He writes of the church that it is "in short, to put it as charitably as possible, a most noble, most venerable superstructure. But what happens to poor Christ Himself within such an edifice? It is clear that ingenuousness, once lost, cannot easily be recovered, and cannot even be regretted decently. Can one pretend that it is still there to be recaptured; can one, after the experience of seeing

² *Encounter*, XXXI, 35-38.

from outside, go back to a pretence of accepting a system of dogmas, in which one no longer recognizes an absolute validity? To do so would be not only a defiance of reason, but also a profanation of one's conscience, a lie to oneself and to others, and offence towards God. Nobody can ask this of a man; no promise, no threat, no well-intentioned pressure can impose it on him. But fortunately, Christ is greater than the Church." [3]

The other example is very different. It is the so-called "Death of God Theology." We might have expected that the idea of the death of God would have undermined the position of Jesus in the beliefs of its exponents. But this is far from being the case. The denial of God, far from ending in a denial of any special claims for Jesus, ends in the assertion that Jesus does matter and matters in a quite peculiar way: that it is Jesus we see when we look out on the world. In discussing the "Death of God Theologies Today," William Hamilton writes: "First, Jesus may be concealed in the world, in the neighbour, in this struggle for justice, in that struggle for beauty, clarity, order. Jesus is in the world as masked, and the work of the Christian is to strip off the masks of the world to find him, to stay with him and to do his work. . . . There is another form of the presence of Jesus Christ in the world. Here, we no longer talk about unmasking Jesus, . . . we talk about becoming Jesus in and to the world. Here, the Christian life, ethics, love, is first a decision about the self, and then a movement beyond the self into the world." [4]

[3] *Ibid.*, p. 62.
[4] Thomas J. J. Altizer and William Hamilton, *Radical Theology and the Death of God* (Indianapolis: Bobbs-Merrill, 1966), pp. 60-61.

## What Name Do We Give Him Now?

Neither of these examples could be said to express commonly held views, though what they are saying would find echoes in the unexpressed thoughts of many people. These examples are given, not because they are in any way representative, but because they show how humanists who reject the church and theologians who reject God do not reject Jesus because he is the symbol of the church and the image of God, but instead see him as possessing for them and for their view of the world an enduring and overriding importance. We might speculate on how this has happened. We certainly can say that this interest reflects the hold that Jesus has on the imaginations of multitudes of people right outside the church. He is the best-known person that has ever lived. The picture that many people have of him may often be simple and sometimes absurd. Some may project upon him their own protest or their own hopes. But it is always a recognizable picture.

But how do men describe him? How do they see him? Despairingly, as the supreme and everlasting example of human sufferings, as the one hope for men if only they would follow him, as the key to the meaning of life, or just as Man, the highest form of life that this earth has produced? We may be tempted to say: What does it matter what the prejudiced, the unsophisticated, the ignorant say about Jesus? Let those who know the Bible and have studied theology say who he is. If those of us who think we have the answers maintain that our opinions should come first, we should remember that Jesus asked his first disciples, "Whom do people say I am?" before he asked them, "Whom do you say that I am?" (Luke 9:18, 20.) What people say of him does matter, if only to force us to describe him also in our own words.

Peter's reply can never be ours now. It was quite definite, even though he may have been surprised to hear himself say it. He gives Jesus the name of "the Christ." Mark's Gospel, the oldest, gives his answer in its simplest form: "Thou art the Christ" (Mark 8:29). Luke gives the answer as "The Christ of God" (Luke 9:20). Matthew adds a little more to it: "Thou art the Christ, the Son of the living God" (Matthew 16:16). By his use of the title "the Christ" Peter meant that Jesus was the man whom the Jews had long expected would be sent by God to deliver them from their enemies and to lead them into their glorious national future. Jesus accepts the name. He says that its use was an inspired guess on Peter's part. His interpretation of the name would be quite different from what the people meant and even Peter expected: so different indeed that Jesus told them not to use it outside. But the name does not mean anything to us today. We do indeed use it as another and even more common name for Jesus. Indeed we use it as if it were his surname. We can accept it as the earliest title for him and should treat it with the serious study it deserves. But it cannot be our answer to Jesus' question. A title that has to be explained historically and linguistically is not a title that we can be said to give.

Words are only symbols—ways of expressing our experience in useful signs. Titles, if they mean anything, are brief descriptions of how we see people. They have great influence on our ways of thinking about people and our way of treating them. But our faith does not lie in the words we use. We have to be careful that the words we use express for ourselves and to other people what we want them to say. Words should help us understand each other. They can also hinder. And this is perhaps especially true of the words we use about Jesus. For these words do not mean today what they meant to earlier generations. They have acquired quite new associations.

In previous centuries men have been more than happy to give authoritarian titles to Jesus. Men have seen nothing incongruous in greeting Jesus as "King of kings and Lord of lords." And we still in much of our worship and prayers address God as if he were an Eastern potentate on his throne. Today we are more than suspicious of dictators, emperors, tyrants, kings. Unless bemused in a haze of medieval worship we would never think of applying such offensive titles to Jesus. And to those outside they seem comic.

The most commonly used title given to Jesus in our worship and in our innocent oaths is that of Lord—"Good Lord." What does the title "Lord" mean to us today? What does it mean in America where the only lord known to men is the landlord? What does it mean in Britain where, to quote Field Marshall Montgomery, lords are "two a penny." And if our English usage has become so familiar that it has lost all meaning, what do we make of it in French and German? *Le Seigneur* suggests the courtier rather than Jesus the carpenter of Nazareth. And *Herr* has other associations, especially with the idea of *Herrenvolk*. *Herr, Seigneur,* Lord —these seem the oddest of names to apply to Jesus. They are political in their implications and a bit repugnant to us today.

The religious titles that past ages have given to Jesus are not much better today. Prophet, priest, savior, redeemer— what do they mean to men today? If they mean anything— and of course they mean a great deal to those of us who have been brought up in the atmosphere and peculiar language of the church—it is as we think ourselves back into the utterly different situation of men a long time ago. For instance the title of redeemer becomes alive when we in our hearts and minds realize a little of what slavery meant in the world of the Roman Empire into which Paul went, when it was the basis of economic life and when the one, almost unrealizable, hope of a slave was that he might be bought with a price and so attain freedom. Redeemer was an inevitable title to give at the time of its first use. The secular world forced it on the church. But it has become archaic and therefore as meaningless as social titles like "Esquire" and "Sir." They reflect something of acquaintance and something of respect. Perhaps they say more about the person who uses them than of the person to whom they are addressed. But they don't have any descriptive meaning for men today. The name we give to Jesus should be intelligible, inevitable, and with immediate challenge to our actions in the world in which we live.

Are there other names that men have used and we have forgotten? "Teacher," for instance. Are there names that Jesus seemed prepared to use of himself but which his followers have never dared to use: as, for instance, "Servant."

## What Name Do We Give Him Now?

Or are there new names that would better describe how we see him than any names used in the past?

Do we need to give him a title at all? Is his own name of "Jesus" not enough?

Is it our place to choose?

# A Question We Must Answer for Ourselves

There is no possibility of finding a final title for Jesus or a final description of him. An orthodox answer becomes a dead answer. Only a fallible, contemporary answer can be a living description of a person. Our names for Jesus must change from age to age. But Jesus remains the same, because he is a person. As the author of the Letter to the Hebrews puts it "Jesus Christ is the same today as he was yesterday and as he will be for ever." (Hebrews 13: 8.) It is the person who is the same, not the name given to him. Here we touch the mystery of personality. A person is the same person however his situation changes and however our knowledge of

22

him grows and however much he himself may develop in understanding and experience. It is with a man who lived his life in this world and still confronts us in the world that men today are concerned when we talk about Jesus. It is on him that the life of the church is built. But how we understand him and how we describe him do not remain the same. This is because our ways of living our lives change. Our ways of thinking about things change and our ways of describing them change. And the way Jesus affects us changes. Our understanding of him changes too. This should not surprise us. The way a child describes his mother is quite different from the way in which he will speak of her when he is grown. She remains the same person, and his love for her has not changed. If we regard anyone as a person and not as a functionary useful to us—and that is how we can regard a Savior or a Redeemer—we are always thinking about him and we change the words in which we talk about him, because they are always quite inadequate to express our affection and understanding. And all the time we know that our words never paint for others the picture we want them to see.

So we are bound in every age to try to find our own name for Jesus, or, if no title quite satisfies, our way of describing him for ourselves and to others. It will be our name for him or our description of him, tentative but intelligible to us and to our contemporaries. But it will not be final. We shall not be able to say that this is the final, the only, name for Jesus and that every attempt to change it will be wrong. For this is not the way we can ever talk about a person. You cannot pigeon-hole a living person.

There is, therefore, no blasphemy in our regarding as inadequate for us today the biblical names given to Jesus in the gospels or the titles given to him by the early church, or names made familiar and dear to us by centuries of prayer and worship. It is right that we should try to understand what the first users of a name meant when they gave it to Jesus. And in our worship we are justified in using these older names in the hymns and prayers of other ages so long as we remember that we are probably translating them in our own minds into more intelligible pictures for ourselves, and realize that they are meaningless to people outside the church. For example, the name "Christ" has never been translated into English. It is a Greek word meaning "anointed" and was used to translate a Hebrew word "Messiah" that also means "anointed." Is that what we mean today when we talk about Christ? We know what we mean by the adjective "Christian." It has quite a different meaning. It means for us today "having the attributes that we see in Jesus." If we are to see Jesus for ourselves and if we are to help other people to see him we must get away from the use of technical words that are quite unintelligible to those who have not specialized in the study of them. We have also to remember that our common words in daily use change their meaning through the years. A word that a former century used with a good meaning, such as "pretender" can become a word we would not like to have applied to ourselves.

But there is another reason why we need to think out for ourselves the names we give to Jesus and the ways in which we describe him. And this is a more important reason. And it is this: Jesus never gave himself a name or title. He never told men what to call him. The twelve disciples, from the beginning of their time with him, must have discussed among themselves what kind of man he really was and how they should speak of him to other people. Was he a prophet, the successor to John the Baptist, and likely to suffer the same fate? Was he the expected national savior who would lead their people to liberty, the successor of many who had brought disaster to themselves and disillusionment to the people? Would he succeed where they had failed? That it was along this latter line that their thoughts moved is evident not only from Peter's confession at Caesarea Philippi but the question they ask after the Resurrection: "Has the time come? Are you going to restore the kingdom to Israel?" (Acts 1:6.) But they never asked him straight out who he was. Perhaps they had learned that he did not answer such questions but had a disconcerting habit of turning the question back on the questioner, as when he said to the man who asked for his help in getting his share of his inheritance: "Who made me a judge or a divider over you?" (Luke 12:14.)

It was Jesus who asked them the question: "Whom do you say that I am?" It was an honest, open question. There is no impression that they ought to have known some correct answer or that Jesus was nudging them into giving the answer he wanted. He accepted the title that Peter gave him of "the Christ." Was this how Jesus thought of himself? Or was this the nearest approximation to what he was doing that he could expect his disciples to give? But what he goes on to say is more significant. He explains that he accepts

25

the title in quite a different sense from that which Peter intended. He tells them to be careful not to use the title when speaking to others. He says that he will not be a victorious national conqueror but that he· will be put to death by the leaders of the people. And, more significantly, he says that if they accept him as Christ they will need to carry out the work of Christ on his terms. He emphasizes the cross they will have to bear, not the one he himself will carry. If they acknowledge him as Christ they themselves will have to act as Christ to other men (Mark 8:29-35).

Apart from this one occasion they never used the title "Christ" of him. They never addressed him so or talked of him so. This does not appear to be how they thought of him as they walked through the fields or sailed with him in their boats and ate and argued among themselves and listened to him and talked until they fell asleep.

The disciples at most times and other men at various times addressed him by other simpler titles. But his reaction to these titles was the same. He accepted them and turned their implication back on those who used them.

The commonest name that his contemporaries gave Jesus was that of "Master." This was the customary title of respect given to a teacher or a superior, just as a polite student will address his professor as "Sir." It meant as much and as little. When it was used with more particular emphasis Jesus questioned its use. When a man addressed him as "Good Master" Jesus retorted "Why do you call me good?" (Mark 10:18.) Even when, according to John's Gospel, he accepted the title "Ye call me Master and Lord: and ye say well, for so I am," he added a pungent word that sent the implication of so addressing him back on them: "If I then, your Lord and Master, have washed your feet, ye also ought to wash one another's feet." This giving him a title did not affect or change him. But it did affect them. It committed them, not him. It was their business, not his.

His enemies did not give him a title, except the more religious of them. They, with the customary reaction of their kind, attributed his work to the devil and called him "Son of Beelzebub" (Matthew 10:25). But they did ask him who he was. They put leading questions to him and suggested names on which they could accuse him. His method with them was the same as with his friends. He did not challenge the title they suggested but put the responsibility of using it back on them.

At his trial Pilate asked him: "Are you the King of the Jews?" In Mark, Matthew, and Luke, Jesus' answer is simple and the same: "You say it." It's as if he were saying: "It is you who bring this title up. You give it to me. It is your doing, not mine." In John's Gospel, Jesus adds the words: "Do you say this of yourself or did others tell it you of me?" (Mark 15:2; Matthew 27:11; Luke 23:3; John 18: 34.) Jesus does not deny the title and it is this title that is superscribed on the cross on which he was crucified: "This is Jesus the King of the Jews" (Matthew 27:37). It was the title given by Pilate in irony, and it was never used of Jesus again.

Before the High Priest, Jesus deals with the question put to him in a slightly different manner. The High Priest asked him if he is "the Christ, the Son of the Blessed." (Mark 14: 61.) In Matthew the question is put more forcibly: "I adjure

27

thee by the living God that thou tell us whether thou be the Christ, the Son of God?" (Matthew 26: 63.) Jesus answered simply "I am." But according to the first three Gospels he adds that they will see the Son of man sitting on the right hand of power and coming in the clouds of heaven. This is a reference to the prophecy of Daniel (7:13). When the High Priest used the title "Christ" Jesus knew what he meant. When Jesus quoted Daniel, the High Priest thought he knew what Jesus meant. Jesus knew that he faced immediate death. He would not die misunderstood by the leaders of his people. He had already told them that if they wanted to inquire about his actions and his teaching they had only to ask the common people. They understood him. If the leaders were befogged in their theological thinking then he had to speak their language. It is significant that he replies to their accusation of claiming to be Son of God by quoting Daniel's prophecy of "Son of Man." As in the other instances in which he uses the words "Son of Man" his reference is to those who suffer for men or to suffering humanity. On these terms he is willing to accept the title "Christ" and is prepared to die. But what he stands for and is prepared to die for is the eternal truth of God. The power of suffering humanity is the power of God in the world and will ultimately be seen as such.

This is the one occasion on which Jesus accepted a title openly but as always he did not leave it there. His questioners have to face its implications for themselves. He was explicit because it was the last question put to him. But what he was asserting was not his claim to a title but the truth of the life he lived. He did not at the end accept a title that before he had hidden from men. Rather at the end and before his enemies he was witnessing to the truth of the life to which he called men. He did so in terms that they could understand, and it infuriated them. His teaching was not about himself or the titles he might claim. It was not even basically about God and His attributes. It was about life— men's life, the life through which they knew God, the life he himself lived and for which he died, life that was victorious in death, life that was eternal, just because it was life, and, therefore, God's. He was not trying to hide anything from men. He said that he had told them all that he knew and he knew that it was the truth of God (John 15: 15). But generally, in his desire to get men to understand and to enter into the life which he was living, and to which he called them, he deflected interest from the titles that men gave him.

They, however, when they got to discussing the life he lived and what it meant had to use words to describe what he was doing and the kind of life he was living. They talked about him as a teacher. At least they talked about him as spending much of his time in teaching. Luke in his Gospel saw teaching as Jesus' main work. The people are reported as regarding him as a teacher but not like the teachers they knew. And yet they called him a teacher. Today we hesitate to call Jesus a teacher. Despite our dependence on education, "teacher" is not a popular name with which to address someone. The word "teaching" evokes the idea of instruction and superiority. We still think of teaching as the kind of instruction in which the Scribes and Pharisees engaged. In our common speech and thinking we have not come to appreciate the changes in the understanding of education and the changed idea of what a teacher is. Dr. Dorothee Sölle in her argument that we see Jesus best when we see him as a teacher says this: "A teacher who does not efface himself, does not remove himself, make himself superfluous, is not a good teacher." [1] The teaching of Jesus was not instruction. He did not give his disciples words to learn. His teaching was not about himself. He did not make them swear loyalty to him. He asked them questions, which they, not he, had to answer, if they could. He made them question everything they had been brought up to accept. He made them think for themselves. He was leading them to do things, and things that always involved other people —loving, forgiving, suffering. He got them to do things together. They had the wit to recognize him as a teacher of an utterly new kind. The church, strangely, has never called him a teacher. It has reserved that title for those who taught as the Scribes.

The disciples also saw him as one who healed people. His reference to the proverb "Physician, heal thyself" may indicate that men thought of him and perhaps addressed him as a physician. Certainly they made use of him as one. And when Jesus sent his disciples out to do his work, it was in teaching and in healing that they were to be employed. This must have been how his contemporaries saw Jesus himself as employing his time. Later when Peter wanted to remind the Jews of what Jesus was like he described him as one "who went about doing good" (Acts 10:38), for this

[1] Dorothee Sölle, *Christ the Representative* (London: SCM Press, 1967), p. 116.

30

is how the common people saw him. Some of his actions of teaching and healing reminded men of the prophets, but there was this great difference, that he did not divide himself off from men, or retreat into the desert, but shared their common life.

But it was his own distinctive life that he shared with them. And of this life that he was living and which he called all men to share he gave vivid pictures, which indirectly describe Jesus himself. He saw forgiveness as the basis of this life and of all human life. He told men to love their enemies and to return evil with good. Clearly they saw him as exemplifying this new life in all that he did and in many instances doing it very dramatically. But though obviously they admired him they felt that this life was not for them. Jesus, however, would never make any unique claim for himself. Forgiveness was the way for everyone. He was talking about life and not about himself. He offset their ordinary use of the word "master" when addressing him by describing his life and all life in terms of a servant. "Ye know that the princes of the Gentiles exercise dominion over them and they that are great exercise authority upon them. But it shall not be so among you: but whosoever will be great among you let him be your servant." (Matthew 20:25-26) And in Luke (22:27) "For whether is greater, he that sitteth at meat or he that serveth? but I am among you as he that serveth." Jesus' emphasis on his role as a servant is disguised for us by its common translation "minister," which has now acquired associations of status and authority. In his use of the word "servant" was he rectifying the balance from their

31

excessive desire for authority? Was he really claiming equality for all men and for himself?

Then again his constant use of the word "brother" to describe the relations that men should have with each other and his talk of those who do the will of God as a family would seem to indicate that he wanted men to see him and treat him as one who shared their life completely. He did not use language that indicated any difference from them except in the willingness of his identification with them. Jesus showed himself as one of them, their brother, who sent them out, as members of the family, to serve others. He made demands on them but they were the demands that a member of a family can make on other members, without apology and without authority. "He makes the largest possible demands on the loyalty, trust and obedience of his followers. And he does this without in any way lording it over them." [2] This emphasis on a family relationship made so strong an impression that the writers of the New Testament often refer to it. Paul in Romans (8: 29) refers to him as "the firstborn among many brethren" and the author of Hebrews says "he is not ashamed to call them brethren," or as the Jerusalem Bible translates it "he openly calls them brothers."

But we never read in the Gospels of the disciples openly calling Jesus brother or treating him as their servant. What held them back? Was it the habit of centuries? Or a sense of their own inferiority? Was it respect and a certain sense

<hr />

[2] Thomas W. Manson, *The Teaching of Jesus* (Cambridge University Press, 1935) pp. 210-11.

of awe? Was it, perhaps, even the fear of what such intimacy with him would lead them into?

It is not a light thing to assume the equality of calling someone your brother. It is now, for us in this age, a difficult thing to call someone our servant. The Chinese habit of asserting in speech the inevitable superiority of everyone else and of all their possessions may be hypocritical but it eases social contacts. The Quaker custom of calling everyone equally a friend can assert an equality that is far from self-denying.

So the Twelve did not address Jesus or speak of him as "brother" "friend" or "servant." We in the church today have become accustomed to hearing him called "brother" and "friend," as in the prayer of St. Richard of Chichester "O most merciful Redeemer, Friend and Brother." But with the disciples, we'd hesitate to call him "servant." There have been those in every age in the church who have delighted to do the most menial tasks: sometimes out of pure love, sometimes to shame themselves and sometimes to make other people feel uncomfortable. But our reluctance to address Jesus as "servant" may reveal a healthy doubt as to whether we have a right to call any man our servant. While we would regard brotherhood and friendship as patterns of human relationships which we have to hold to and develop, we would never give the same unquestioned validity to the relationship of master and servant. If we are to retain the word servant as in any sense a title for Jesus or for a Christian, we shall need to use it differently, without its old idea of subjection and with a new idea of freedom. Is this how Jesus himself used it? What did

Jesus mean when he said that he came as one who serves? Have we any word that expresses his meaning adequately?

Perhaps the key to the picture that Jesus wanted men to have of him and of the life he was living is to be found in his use of the word "friend" when he said at the end of his life: "Henceforth I call you not servants; for the servant knoweth not what his lord doeth; but I have called you friends; for all things that I have heard of my Father I have made known unto you." (John 15:15.) Friendship involves a knowledge of what each does and an acceptance of it. And this, perhaps, explains why Jesus was reluctant to accept any title that men wanted to give him. The more important thing was that they should understand the life he was living and accept it.

He was leading them into a new way of life together. It would not be a new way of life—it certainly would not be his way of life—if men entered it in blind obedience, as servants, or in complete misunderstanding of its demands. They could only live his kind of life if they knew what they were doing and wanted to do it and enjoyed doing it. He was leading men into a new liberty, free of domination and equal in the demands that men could make of each other. The titles that men give each other either have an original emphasis of status and authority or acquire these through use, because freedom and the responsibility of equality are things they usually want to avoid. And one way of avoiding them for ourselves is to land them on other people to whom we give titles in recompense.

This nonauthoritarian attitude of Jesus to other men reflects his knowledge of God. Jesus never gave any direct teaching about God. He never gave men categorical instruction about what God was like or how he acted. To give authoritarian teaching about God is an expression of our own desire to exercise authority. Jesus' words about God are never of this kind. His teaching about God is thrown off in asides, in pictures and in questions. This is perhaps the only way we can ever talk about God. We can only very hesitatingly interpret our experience of God. Jesus did not indeed hesitate in his few words about God. His pictures are more definite than any definition. But he refused to elaborate, interpret, or modify his surprising pictures. For what is his picture of God? God clothes the flowers of the field and prepares meals for sparrows. He makes the sun to rise on the evil and the good—indiscriminately. He sends his rain on the just and the unjust. He is like a working man who works overtime and on Sundays (John 5:16-17). The pictorial language that Jesus uses is a sign that he is not arguing with people, for then he would use their language. He is expressing the certainty of his own personal experience. He is saying that God is concerned with life; with all that makes for life, with love and not hate, with forgiveness and not punishment. God never learns from experience but, however man reacts, goes on taking the same risks. He did indeed speak about God as his father and as their father. But the picture he gave of what their father was like shocked his hearers by its lack of paternal authority. Jesus' real blasphemy in the eyes of the Pharisees was not that he made himself equal to God but that he made God like himself. And this was why Paul declared that Jesus was the image of God.

Jesus was opening to men a new way of life that was revolutionary and challenging, attractive and terrifying. One of the reasons why they drew back from giving him the names that he seemed willing to accept, such as friend, brother, and servant, was that to do so would be to commit them to this new way of life expressed in these names.

The names we, down the ages, have rejoiced to give to Jesus have often hidden him from us. They put him in a position from which he always escapes. They have made him a very shadowy person for many, just as the names that we have so freely given to God in the past have made the very idea of God unreal to many today. Any name for God takes something from the mystery which is the only way that we can think of God. It may be that our contemporary questioning of our inherited ideas of God and our questioning of our inherited patterns of social and political life are getting us nearer to an understanding of what Jesus was doing and what he was talking about and even of how he thought of God. At least we are now in that open, uncomfortable, yet invigorating situation in which he put his contemporaries.

All the names given to Jesus in his life on earth were given by his contemporaries. To him none seemed to be adequate, or was accepted unquestioningly except the name given to him by Joseph at his birth—Jesus. This name gave him his place in society and showed men who he was: "Is not this Joseph's son?" (Luke 4:22) "Is not this the carpenter's son?" (Matthew 13:55) It was the name the people used, sometimes with the addition of the name of his home: Jesus of Nazareth; and sometimes with a reference to his family: Son of David. Jesus was his name just as Tom, Dick, or Harry may be your name; the name that distinguishes you. Perhaps it is the only satisfactory name for us to use. But do we know him well enough to use it?

# Can We Call Him Lord? Lord of What?

But, of course, if you are going to talk about someone to people who don't know him, you can't just call him Tom or Dick or Harry, or Jesus. You hope that they will get to know him well enough to call him by his own name. But they will never want to know him unless you excite their curiosity and make them feel that they would like to meet him. You have to give some kind of description of him. You have to use some word or set of words that gives an indication of what kind of person he is and what he does. You have to say that Tom is worth meeting because he is an amusing talker; or Dick because he plays football well; or Harry because he is a TV personality; or Jesus because he is . . . what?

How do we describe Jesus to men today?

The early church faced this question when they moved out of their indigenous situation in Jerusalem. So long as they stayed there and talked to those who lived in Jerusalem and its environs, they did not need to use any other name than that of Jesus. When they met with friends in their own homes and when they talked with strangers in the streets they were speaking to those who had either seen and heard Jesus or at least had heard about him and of his teaching and about the scandal of his trial and death. They did not have to add any title to describe him. They used the name by which men had spoken of him before—Jesus of Nazareth. They wanted to talk about him and about nothing else. They talked about him as one who had been cruelly killed and whom they knew to be somehow miraculously still alive. But they wanted specially to remind those who had seen him of what he had been like and what he had done, and to correct the other stories that gossip spread. And to those who had never seen him they wanted to excite their curiosity. The descriptive words they used all revived the memory of the man they knew, whose life they had shared.

At Pentecost, Peter spoke to the people of Jesus as "Jesus of Nazareth, a man approved of God among you by miracles and wonders and signs, which God did by him in the midst of you, as you yourselves also know; him . . . ye have taken, and by wicked hands have crucified and slain; whom God hath raised up" (Acts 2:22-24).

To Cornelius, who as a foreigner inquired about the faith,

Peter described Jesus as one "who went about doing good, and healing all that were oppressed of the devil; whom they slew and hanged on a tree: Him God raised up" (Acts 10:38-40).

In the prayer in which the Christians in Jerusalem gave thanks for the release of Peter and John, Jesus is twice referred to as "thy holy child Jesus" (Acts 4:27, 30). The New English Bible and the Jerusalem Bible translate the word as "servant." Perhaps the best translation would be the word "boy" in the old colonial sense. It is hard to believe that we have in this passage the exact record of their corporate prayer. But these words give an indication of how these early Christians thought of Jesus as one who was young and in a subordinate position. They could see him as Lord and Christ (Acts 4:26; 2:36). But the starting point was Jesus and the kind of life he lived. However exalted was the language in which they described him now, he was still this youth, "this same Jesus" (Acts 2:36).

Doubtless at this stage they had not thought out all that their experience would mean for them. It was enough that they had known Jesus and knew that he was alive. It meant for them that they were freed from that fear of separation and of death that had made them so jealous of one another and had made them cling so closely to Jesus, and made them demand so much for themselves from him. They knew, now, that their relationship was liberated from those jealousies and ambitions and fears which arise from our conviction that our relations with others are at the mercy of separation and of other people, of distance and death. They knew that they were in a free and eternal relationship to

Jesus and to each other and, indeed, to all men. This was what made them appear drunk with excitement and bold to act. They did not try to think out an explanation of all this. The experience was enough.

They insisted that all that mattered was Jesus—the man he was, the life he lived, the death he died. They were not reminding their contemporaries of the sad story of some youth who was now dead. They were asserting that Jesus had opened their eyes to what life was all about now and forever. It was in his name that life was to be found. And his name was simply Jesus.

But this name was not adequate when they moved out of Jerusalem into the wider world. They had to use other words to describe Jesus to those who did not know the background and the gossip of Jerusalem. It was not an easy task. They had to use another language. They had to take strange words with different basic meanings and with very different associations and use them to express ideas which were difficult enough to express in their own language. So Paul took the language of slavery, which was the basic and familiar fact of life in the Roman world but strange to the Jews, as the best means of showing to those of the Roman world what their experience of liberty meant. But "redeemer"—the one who had paid a price to set slaves free— was not the commonest or the earliest title they gave to Jesus to describe him to those outside.

The gospel they proclaimed in Jerusalem might be said to be stated in the two words "Jesus is." What they proclaimed was the eternal fact and significance of Jesus. In these two words was expressed the simple magnitude of the gospel. But questions would follow. Men would ask, as we have asked, "If Jesus is, what then is he? How would you describe him? What did he do?" In a way all our descriptions are embroideries which take away from the simplicity of "Jesus is." To be a Christian all that we need is to know him and to know that he is. But to talk about him and to get others to know him we need to use words that bring him down to human understanding. To the Jews in Jerusalem the apostles had to add the words "Lord" and "Christ": "Jesus is Lord and Christ." To the outside world "Christ" meant nothing. But they kept the title "Lord." "Jesus is Lord" became the first confession of the church's faith.

They kept the word "Lord" because it came to them from the Old Testament with a wealth of meaning; but also because it was easily translated into other languages. All ancient societies had their ideas of lordship. And it is still the title we most commonly use of Jesus: in our worship, in our prayers, in our hymns, and in our common speech. It has for us the authority of the Bible and the associations of centuries. It is doubtful whether in the Roman world it was used with any more precise meaning than the words "Sir" and "Mister" are used by us today. It is doubtful, too, what we think we mean by it today.

To the early church it was not merely a term of respect; an acknowledgment that Jesus was their leader. To the Jews it had a much more precise meaning. "Lord" was not just the description of a person or a title of respect. It always related the one so named to the material world, to a place. You could not have a lord in the abstract, just by himself and for himself. When in Acts 10:36 Peter said of Jesus "He is Lord of all," he was being more accurate than when he said simply that Jesus is Lord. A lord must have his dominion, his possession.

This is true also of our English word "Lord." It meant originally the giver of bread, because the Lord was the owner of the land and responsible for its use. A lord had to have land. This is seen in our use of the Scots form of the word *laird*. If a man sells his land, the title of *laird* goes to the new owner with the land. He cannot keep the title of *laird* once he has given up the land. In our modern English usage the connection of lordship with land has been broken. A lord can sell his land and yet retain his territorial title.

The biblical use of the word "lord" had this basic connection with land but it went much deeper. The basic belief of the Bible is that there is only one Lord and he is God. The Jews must acknowledge no other lord. And no man could call himself lord. No individual could claim absolute possession of land for himself. The sins against which the prophets fulminated were that men claimed the right to do what they liked with their possessions and that they allowed other gods to have dominion over them. This idea of God as not only the creator but the possessor of the earth and therefore the giver of bread is all through the Old Testament and shines through everything that Jesus says: in his prayer "Give us this day our daily bread" and in his attitude to and teaching on what we like to call "our possessions."

When, therefore, the early church called Jesus "Lord," they were making a quite stupendous claim for him. They were saying that Jesus was in the same relation to the material world as God is. And when the Jews talked in this way they did not mean only that God had acted in the beginning to get the whole thing going. They meant far more that there was a continuous creative purpose at work in the world and that this was supremely manifest in men's history.

The early Christians were not so naïve as to think that Jesus, the man whom they knew, was now the manipulator of all the actions of the universe. What they knew was that they were, to quote the words of Ronald Gregor Smith, "liberated from magic spells and from incomprehensible authority." [1]

When these early Christians thus acclaimed Jesus as "Lord" they were declaring that they saw the meaning of life in him—for themselves and for all men, and for all material things. They now knew what the purpose and the glory of the world was. They knew that everything—all men and all things—would find their fulfillment in him. But when we wonder at the rhapsody with which Paul describes how "all things in heaven and things on earth and things under the earth" (Phil. 2:10) should be lifted up into final glory, the real wonder lies not in this hope but in the assumption that it is in Jesus, who assumed the condition of a servant and who died on the cross (Phil. 2:7, 8) that the meaning of everything, and the final glory are to be found. But men are directly implicated. The passage and the argument start from the claim. "In your minds you must be the same as Christ Jesus." Jesus for them held the key to life. He was the way, the truth, and the life. He was

---

[1] Ronald Gregor Smith, *The Free Man* (London: Collins, 1969), p. 21.

the new man, the "firstborn of every creature" and "the image of God." (Col. 1: 15).

When they said that Jesus was Lord, they were saying something very definite about him and something very surprising about the world. Is this what we mean today when we say that Jesus is Lord? Is this our view of the world? I suppose our great difficulty, if we are honest, is that we find it very difficult to see Jesus in relation to the world at all. At bottom this is because we find it difficult to relate ourselves to the material world. We live in the world. We are dependent on the world. We try to understand its laws. We adjust ourselves to its conditions. We seem to make the fullest use of its resources. But it is there, immovable, implacable, inexorable in the rigidity of its laws. We may find, and should find, security in its constancy. But we do not feel that the material world could be said to be responsive to the word of Jesus. Charles Wesley could sing "He rules o'er earth and heaven." We would find it difficult to say that literally or rationally.

Our view of the material world began to change radically four hundred years ago. Changes in ways of knowing and thinking take a long time to affect our common speech and opinions. It is probably only in this century, or, to be more particular, in the second half of this century, that this new view of the world has come to be taken for granted—just when many scientists are beginning to say that it is far too simple. This makes it only the more difficult for ordinary men and women today to be clear in their own minds about Jesus' relation to the world or their own relation to the world. As John Robinson asks: "What, for instance, is the reference of such an affirmation like 'Jesus is Lord'? Does such a statement—and by implication all God-talk—tell us something about reality, about how things are? Or does it merely tell us something about the commitment of the person who makes it? " [2]

Part, and a great part, of our difficulty in discussing the world or reality today is that we talk in one way about it and are now beginning to think about it in quite a different way. It has taken four hundred years for a scientific view of the world to begin to affect men's thinking about the world in which they live. By "scientific" I mean the acceptance and the interpretation of all certifiable facts. But we still speak a language that reflects a different view. It is not that only now do men accept facts. Men have always had to base their life on the acceptance of facts—of day and night, summer and winter. But men before our age and men in all other parts of the world have always believed that their life was made up of two types of experience. These might often be said to express different views of life and to be looking opposite ways but they represented, as it were, two sides of the same coin, different in superscription and not easily seen at the same time, but of a piece. The material world might be thought of as a shadow of reality; the shadow reflected in a cave by the light outside, as in Plato's image. Or, at the other extreme, the world might be the very material in which God, the Creator, works and the only means by which men can know him—the image of the potter and the pot as in the Old Testament; but God outside, the

[2] John A. T. Robinson, *Exploration into God* (Stanford University Press, 1967), p. 59.

final reality. And in between these two are the changing patterns of Western man's thinking about the world. The pattern was always one that held two worlds together which in themselves were as opposite as heaven and hell. The pattern was usually expressed in ascending rings or spheres of influence, of light, of the divine. To us today it all seems like a fairy tale. But it is the pattern in which Shakespeare and Milton and all our poets up till Wordsworth thought and wrote; and the way in which the translators of the Authorized Version of the Bible, the editors of the Book of Common Prayer and the great hymn-writers of the eighteenth century thought and wrote. And it is still the basis of our common speech and of our unthinking thinking. Whenever we talk about heaven and "God up there" we are using their language.

It was, I suppose, always, but in differing ways, taken as figurative language but it was taken as the only figurative language that could interpret reality. For us the picture has gone and the language does not help.

But it does remain the setting in which we talk about Jesus as Lord, because our thinking of the lordship of Christ has been and still is so much molded by the language of the Authorized Version and the prayers and hymns of the church. We have broken the unity that held the two sides precariously together. For us who still use the old religious language, heaven and this world now belong to two different orders. And we do not know where to locate the lordship of Jesus. Do we mean that he is lord of the shadowy kingdom of another world? Or do we mean that he is the determining factor in the material world as we describe it now? Is he the sender of earthquake, flood, and drought? To claim either would be ridiculous to modern man. Nor would it at all express what the men of the New Testament meant.

In much of our contemporary talking in the church we seem to be trying to accept the reality of these two worlds—the other world and this material world—by keeping them apart. In a recent book on Christianity and Communism in China, which has otherwise some useful things to say, these sentences appear: "Christ alone is the Lord of history and the author of redemption. He reigns from His throne above the troubled seas of human life. History, which to the uninitiated is a meaningless tangled skein, is in fact an orderly progress towards its glorious consummation when Christ, the Lion of Judah, will reign as King of kings and Lord of lords over all the world." [8] The language is biblical. The ideas are strictly orthodox. But has it anything to do with reality? Is this what we mean by the Lordship of Jesus? Of course we can interpret the picture in all kinds of ways. But does it have anything of hope to say to men and women living and struggling in the world today? Of course this kind of interpretation does offer men a recompense. It is the hope of rest, of escape into another world. The hymn books of last century and of this are so saturated with this idea that it is almost impossible to find a modern hymn that, in Christian sequel to the Psalms, has anything to say about the world as the creation of God and of man's life on earth. The Christian is a stranger in a vale of tears, and Jesus is lord of another world, not of the world he came to save.

[8] Leslie T. Lyall, *Red Sky at Night* (London: Hodder and Stoughton, 1969), p. 7.

## Can We Call Him Lord? Lord of What?

Our task is not to stake out a claim for Jesus in some unexplored territory elsewhere. It is to begin to be concerned with the world we know and of which we are part. It is probably only as we see the world in relation to ourselves that we shall be able to see the relation of Jesus to the world.

However men of today look at the world and from whatever angle, they are unable to accept any kind of duality. They cannot divide reality into that of this world and of another world. They cannot see themselves as persons with two natures. The experiences they have of reality may be very diverse and even contradictory but they know that these are parts of the experience of one person. The problem for us is not to draw a line to divide our experiences into two opposing sections, spiritual and physical, but to find a unity.

This search for a total unity is a distinguishing mark of modern thought. It is a common characteristic of those who seriously approach the problem of understanding the world today and man's life in it even though the ways in which they approach differ and the answers they put forward do not agree.

This conception of unity has, of course, from the beginning been the foundation of any scientific study of the world. Perhaps in the past the area that could be studied scientifically was so circumscribed that much of human experience was left outside. Today scientists would draw the circle much wider and would claim that all human experience must come within the area of ascertainable scientific knowledge. The wider the circle the more certain it is that the world of our experience must be seen as a unity which cannot be divided. In particular the facts of human personality cannot now be excluded.

This scientific outlook has affected our philosophical and theological thinking. Contemporary theological thinking is confusing to many in its diversity. But what is common to all types of theological thinking today is the basic conviction that we can no longer think in dualistic ways. This is as much a stumbling block to many Christians as is the peculiarity of the individual theologian's opinions. The conventional religious language which we have inherited and which is expressed in popular hymns and in many prayers and sermons is far more dualistic in its impact than many of those who use it realize. And, again, we have been trained in the church to think that our duty is to draw lines of division as, for instance, between Christians and non-Christians, Catholics and Protestants, Anglicans and Methodists, between soul and body, church and world, the religious and the secular. The result of both these traditions is to make many feel that an assertion of unity is both an affront to their traditions and a questioning of their basic beliefs. And this is so whether the unity under discussion is the unity of our experience or the unity of the church. But the common spring of all the new theologies is the need to find unity. This is what holds them together. It is, indeed, what gives them their importance. Three modern lines of theological thinking may be mentioned as examples.

There is the line conspicuously represented by Teilhard de Chardin. His approach is that of a scientist—an anthropologist and archaeologist—as well as of a Jesuit trained in theology. His emphasis is on the unity of spirit and matter, of what is experienced within and what is explored without, of the divine and the human. He would explain this unity through the scientific knowledge that is now ours today of the history of the earth and of man's life on it. He would see Christ as the key and the end of the whole process. To many he seems to stand for a kind of scientific mysticism difficult to share. But there is no doubt that his message to men is of unity.

The two other ways of modern theological thinking seem very different. There are, first of all, those who find in the word "secular" the key to unity. They are suspicious of the word "religion" because it seems to imply a division of experience and of the world. They see man's experience as confined to space and time. God can only be known by what happens in space and time. In particular, the Incarnation was an event in space and time. This world of men's history, experience and present life is the world of which it speaks rather than the material world of science. But equally its message is of unity.

The other line is more philosophical or psychological. It is based on the unity of personality and of human experiences. It is concerned with how we know reality and how we interpret our personal, social, and political experience. Perhaps this line is best summed up in Tillich's description of God as "the ground of all being."

All these different lines of thinking emphasize the impossibility of maintaining a dualistic interpretation of the universe. None would accept the reduction of our knowledge of the universe to the field of physical, scientifically measurable facts. All would see that human personality is also an inescapable, if not easily measured, fact. God has not been expelled from the universe. Mystery has been brought in again. New ways are open to our understanding of what we mean by God.

How, then, do we see Jesus in relation to this new unified world that we are trying to get to know today?

Our difficulty in thinking about Jesus in relation to the world is probably due to our thinking in outmoded terms of dominion and power. We cannot see him as in possession of the material world. Some people can perhaps imagine him as in possession of a quite different other world, where he sits at the right hand of God, from which he will come at some unknown future to take possession of this world and judge it. This is not the Jesus we know: "this same Jesus" who lived on earth. If we see this Jesus at all in this world of ours it is apt to be only in his suffering. We see him as we like to see ourselves, as the victims of the world's heartless cruelty. We see this world not only as the scene of the crucifixion but forever displaying Jesus on his cross.

In a review of Simone Weil's *Selected Essays, 1934-1943*,[4] John Wren-Lewis has this to say:

"The new collection of essays by Simone Weil are interesting for the way they reveal the motivation which underlies the reluctance of many religious people to accept the modern outlook. As in all her writings, the reader becomes rapidly aware of a constant warfare between an extremely high intelligence and a masochistic desire to conceive of the

[4] Simone Weil, *Selected Essays, 1934-1943*, Richard Rees, trans. (Oxford University Press, 1962).

universe as a Great System before which the individual must abase himself, at the cost of mortifying all his most human desires. Again and again in the early essays in the book, all of which are on scientific themes, she regrets the modern recognition of science as a tool for getting things done, precisely because it removes the classical picture of a world of iron necessity before which the human spirit must prostrate itself. Like the neurotic returning to his neurosis, she spurns the promise of liberation which modern science, truly understood, offers.

"The fascinating essays in the second half of the book show where her religion really belonged, in the pessimism of Greek thought. 'Our country is the Cross' is the keynote of these essays, but the pioneers who created modern science were able to do so because *they* took from Christianity the message that our country is the resurrection, the dominion of creative personality over Nature in ordinary human life." [5]

If we are to see Jesus in positive relation to the world as we know it today, it must be in terms of personality and of our understanding of the meaning and purpose of the world. No one would claim that this is easy. But no one has ever claimed that faith is easy or that the mystery of life is easy to understand. What we can claim is that it means something and offers challenge and hope. We can no longer talk with any pretense of meaning about God as if he were an oriental despotic ruler of a rebellious kingdom, or of Jesus as his deputy in this kind of rule. We can see Jesus as the key to life, the opener of doors, the creator of new

[5] *The Guardian*, November 1, 1968.

life. We can see him as helping us to a new idea of God and a new trust in his purposes. Such words point to the future and not to the past. The words we use would inevitably be tentative, questioning, demanding, involving us in action and in hope.

This kind of talking would not be very far from what the early Christians meant when they called Jesus Lord. At least, this title, and the other titles that they gave him, pointed to the future rather than the past. When Paul said that Jesus was the firstborn of every creature he was thinking of a new humanity, of men, all men, at last entering into their inheritance. When he went on immediately to call Jesus the image of God he was surely saying, as he does elsewhere, that men would come to see and understand the meaning and purpose of all creation in Jesus and so to understand what it means to call God Father.

And perhaps Paul and the author of the Letter to the Hebrews would have welcomed men's present beginning of the conquest of space. At least they would have understood it better than the theologians of the Middle Ages and of the Reformation, who emphasized man's weakness and impotence and the impudence of his gestures of achievement in face of God's power and eternity. Paul could look forward to the day when all things would find their fulfillment as men together attained their glorious liberty. And the author of the Letter to the Hebrews could regret that in his day he could not see all things put under the foot of man but looked now in confidence to the day when they would be. They would not have seen anything presumptuous in man stepping onto the moon. They might have seen in the risks that men take, their willingness to lay down their lives, the dedication of their skill and their cooperation to the uttermost, signs of the way in which all men and all things find their fulfillment in Jesus. Has this nothing to do with Jesus as the hope of the world?

Whenever we talk of hope we move into a world in which purpose and not origin rules. Hope looks to the future but it has not turned its back on the past. It is the experience of the past that leads us on to hope, for without hope there is no continuity. This is presumably what Paul meant when he said that experience produces hope.

Jürgen Moltmann, the German theologian, says of the titles that the early church gave to the risen Christ that "they were therefore not hard and fast titles which defined who he was and is, but open and flexible titles, so to speak, which announce in terms of promise what he will be. They are therefore at the same time also dynamic titles. They are stirred and stirring ideas of mission, which seek to point men to their work in the world and their hope in the future of Christ." [5]

But what name describes this function of Jesus for us today? "Lord" is misleading and inadequate. It now belongs to the past, to another age. It speaks of possession and authority but not of hope. Perhaps we have to make the hope a bit more real to ourselves and be committed to it in thought and action and continue to do so for some time, before we will know what name is adequate to express to ourselves and others what we know to be true of Jesus.

---

[5] Jürgen Moltmann, *Theology of Hope*, James W. Leitch, trans. (New York: Harper, 1967), p. 202.

# Dare I Call Him "Mine"?

But this has not been the way in which men in the last three hundred years have thought of Jesus. They have thought of him in a much more personal way. They have thought of him as their Savior and their Lord rather than as the Ruler of Nature and Lord of the Earth. This change has been due in some measure to the fact that in the last three hundred years we have come to know a great deal more about the laws that govern nature and have found it much more difficult to think of an

> Eternal Ruler of the ceaseless round
> Of circling planets.

But it has been due much more to the way in which men's interests have turned in upon themselves. Men have been asking questions about their own life as individuals and in societies: about the meaning of life and about human destiny. So men have thought of Jesus in relation to themselves rather than in relation to the material world. The picture of Jesus has lost its cosmic dimension. Jesus has been seen, not as the world's Redeemer but as "my Savior." And the religious questions that men have discussed have been about the meaning of this: about election, about the atonement, about the salvation of the individual. The call to men has been to come to terms with Jesus, to accept his offer of salvation, to enthrone him in their hearts. It is as if we had come to think of Jesus almost as our personal possession. We were even prepared to say that he was ours.

This is a very different picture from that of the early church or from that discussed in the last chapter. But it illustrates the way in which those who have been molded by the teaching and the worship of the church think of Jesus. But it also explains why so many, even in the church, have a very hazy picture of Jesus and cannot find any great relevance in what they are told to believe about him. For men and women in the second half of the twentieth century the picture of Jesus as the Savior of the individual raises as many questions as does that of Jesus ruling from the right hand of God on high. And perhaps they are more difficult questions because they are not merely intellectual. They are moral. And, therefore, the answers men get are not so likely to satisfy them. It is not just the intellectual question of how some can be saved and others not, that puzzles men today. It is rather the moral question as to whether some have any right to expect a destiny denied to others.

This is a far more difficult question to answer because we have not merely to be convinced of it intellectually; we have to accept it morally. Men and women today, with their new sense of their dependence on other people, and their responsibility for them, find it hard to make a personal claim of possession on anyone, including Jesus.

And yet, of course, personal relationship to Jesus in love and obedience is the basis of the Christian life. It goes back to the first disciples and the beginning of it all. It was from their meeting with Jesus and from all that Jesus did with them and to them and for them that the church grew. It was to preserve this knowledge of Jesus for all who had not known him in the flesh that the Four Gospels were written. And always, and sometimes as if by a miracle, the knowledge of Jesus has been there in the church, for without it the church would have become fossilized or have faded quite away. Sometimes it has seemed quite hidden. Sometimes it has needed the assault of violent men to tear away the wrappings and let Jesus be seen. At other, unexpected times, without any obvious reason except that he was there, some men have seen him as if with their own eyes.

But for all that, it has never been easy for men to see Jesus in this way. It would be wrong to assume that down the centuries all members of the church, or even the majority of them, have seen their faith in this way. There have been long stretches of time, and added together perhaps making up most of the church's history, when any sense of Jesus as a person and of a personal relationship to him was dim, if not quite nonexistent. We are today often shocked by the ignorance shown by children at school of the Bible and of the facts of Jesus' life. It is doubtful whether this ignorance is any worse than among the members of the church everywhere in any century in the past, when taken all together. The faith has been presented to men in other ways. Other things have brought people into the church or kept them there; an accepted way of life, fear of being detached from it, a tradition of worship and behavior. The miracle has been that somehow the vision of the person of Jesus has always persisted and at times broken through the traditions of the institution and the trappings of its thought. In the Middle Ages, when everything in man's knowledge seemed to be brought into the adornment of the church except the human person of Jesus himself, there are always unexpected reminders that men saw him, as in the prayer of St. Richard of Chichester:

> O most merciful Redeemer, Friend and Brother,
> May I know thee more clearly,
> Love thee more dearly,
> And follow thee more nearly [1]

and in the knowledge of Jesus shining, often unacknowledged, through the actions and attitudes of Francis of Assisi.

In the sixteenth century the translation of the Bible into the language of the people, the spread of education, the invention of printing, a new concern about children and the family; these all brought knowledge of Jesus into men's minds and hearts. Perhaps in no one is this awareness of

[1] Prayer of Richard of Chichester (c. 1197-1253).

Jesus as a man more obvious than in Martin Luther. His vivid picture of the baby in the manger and the man on the cross seems at times to challenge and to humanize his theological toughness, as when he writes: "When I am told that God became man, I can follow the idea, but I just do not understand what it means. For what man, if left to his natural promptings, if he were God, would humble himself to lie in the feedbox of a donkey or to hang upon a cross." [2] But there is little enough sign of this picture lightening up the aridity of post-Reformation theology. And even in the theology of Luther and Calvin what happened between Bethlehem and Calvary seems disregarded as if "all that Jesus began both to do and teach" and the kind of man he was and the life he lived was of no consequence to the faith. And yet this was what the evangelists set out to tell—"the whole story from the beginning." And this was the man men knew: who was laid in a manger and died on a cross.

In the history of the church it has been through the heretics and the rebels—both those driven out like the Waldenses and those accepted and kept in like the Franciscans—that obedience to Jesus as a person has been brought back into the concern of Christians. This obedience has often been expressed in obscurantist ways: in the literal acceptance of certain verses of the Bible rather than in the understanding of Jesus' teaching as a whole and, in their relations with other people, in extreme bigotry and sectarianism. But without the heretics and the rebels the church

[2] Roland H. Bainton, *Here I Stand: A Life of Martin Luther* (Nashville: Abingdon Press, 1951), p. 173.

might well have become, as it seemed to them to have become and as it seems to the rebels of today to be becoming, an institution concerned solely with its own formation and reformation.

It is, therefore, perhaps surprising that it was not until two hundred years after the Reformation, in the eighteenth century, in an age which for us often seems the arid age of reason, that men began, as it were, to take this picture of Jesus into their daily lives and thinking. They began to search for and to invent new names to describe the Jesus whom they found. They were not afraid to use these new titles. According to a modern scholar these titles are "the most recent of any importance in the history of thought." [3] This is a large claim. Is it justified? What new titles did they find? Why were they bold enough to adopt them?

By the eighteenth century men in Western Europe knew that they were in a new age. The medieval world was gone and almost forgotten, more strange to them then than it is to us now. The theological controversies and the religious wars of the Reformation and the century that followed seemed to them relics of barbarism that should be forgotten. Their interests were more mundane. They were concerned with practical things; with the development of trade and commerce, with the discovery of the new world of America and the old world of China, with the philosophical questions that this discovery of the primitive savage and the sophisticated Chinese raised about the nature of man and his place in the world. After being confined for hundreds

[3] Dorothee Sölle, *Christ the Representative*, p. 116.

of years behind the battlements of Christendom they looked out on a new world with extravagant hopes. Their hopes were political: for the abolition of tyrannies and the preservation and growth of liberties. Their life was domestic. The faith had to find its expression in a domestic, commercial society whose ideal was peace not war.

Men were reacting against the militancy of Christendom. They were reacting against the picture of Jesus as the bearer of a sword, the sign in which men fought and conquered. St. Bernard of Clairvaux, the monk and great leader of the twelfth century, is associated in our minds with hymns attributed to him like

> Jesus, the very thought of thee
> With sweetness fills the breast

But he was known to the men of his time, and to history, as the inspirer of the Second Crusade, its main recruiting sergeant. When he called Jesus

> King most wonderful,
> Thou conqueror renowned

he was not using pictorial language. He was thinking of war. At the success of his recruiting of men for the Crusade, he wrote in exultation to the Pope: "I opened my mouth: I spoke: and at once the Crusaders are multiplied to infinity. Villages and towns are now deserted. You will scarcely find one man for every seven women. Everywhere you see widows whose husbands are still alive." [4] Men of the eighteenth

[4] Steven Runciman, A *History of the Crusades*, II (Cambridge University Press, 1952), p. 254.

century rejected this picture of Jesus. Men of the eighteenth
century were also reacting against the other picture of Jesus
that dominated the later Middle Ages—the dying body on
the cross. It may be that men felt that they had escaped from
the butchery of the Middle Ages, when death was always
near through war, famine, and plague. Perhaps they did
not wish to face the tragedy of life. They were more anxious
to advance its comfort and to enjoy its ease. Certainly they
did not want to keep before them a picture of Jesus that
was the emblem of suffering, death, and defeat. It may have
suited a Europe that had known only too well suffering,
death, and defeat, but they felt it did not suit them.

They wanted to see Jesus differently. They had to see him
differently if he was to be relevant to their society. They had
to see him afresh if he was to mean anything to them personally.

The men who found the new names and gave them to
the church were the hymn-writers in England, Charles Wesley, John Newton, James Montgomery, with Isaac Watts
as the link with the previous century but also tentatively
finding new names for Jesus, as in the original second line
of his most famous hymn:

> When I survey the wondrous Cross
> Where the young prince of glory died.

It is significant that it was in hymns that these new titles
appeared. The painters of the previous centuries had
painted the events of the Gospels against a contemporary
background, Italian or Dutch, and had helped men to see
Jesus in human terms. But hymns for use in worship and

the home are both more intellectual and more massively influential. They put words into people's mouths and made them think. Bernard Manning says of Wesley's Hymn Book of 1779: "This little book—some 750 hymns—ranks in Christian literature with the Psalms, the Book of Common Prayer, the Canon of the Mass." [5] These books have all affected the thinking and living of millions of people and helped generations of Christians to participate in worship. What is unique about the hymns is that they enabled men and women to see Jesus personally perhaps for the first time and certainly in a new light. The hymns got them together to sing about Jesus. This was new. And this movement was not confined to England. It was as evident in Germany.

The titles that they gave to Jesus were many. They recovered old names and they found new ones. "They began to use hitherto unfamiliar or little used titles such as Friend, Teacher, Physician, Advocate, Founder—peaceful, civilized titles after a long period dominated by terms like Hero and Warrior." [6]

Instead of looking at a catalogue of names used in hundreds of hymns, let us look more closely at one hymn that is both typical and familiar to most people—John Newton's

> How sweet the Name of Jesus sounds
> In a believer's ear!

---

[5] Bernard L. Manning, *The Hymns of Wesley and Watts* (London: Epworth Press, 1942), p. 14.

[6] Sölle, *Christ the Representative*, pp. 12, 13.

### Dare I Call Him "Mine"?

It begins, as so many of the hymns we are considering do, with the simple name of Jesus. The name is the starting point. The name is the subject. And the name is Jesus. Then after describing what the mere mention of the name does for him, he goes on in the third verse, to try out new titles for Jesus. In the first line, after repeating the name "Jesus" he gives three titles with a personal emphasis:

> Jesus, my Savior, shepherd, friend,

In the next line he goes back to traditional titles, the *munus triplex*, the three conventional descriptions of Jesus' office in scholastic theology, but he prefixes them with the word "my":

> My prophet, priest, and king,

as if the word "my" redeemed the titles in an age that questioned the right of kings and was very suspicious of priests. He then goes on, still with the prefix "my" to try some new experimental titles, more general and social in content, and all biblical:

> My Lord, my life, my way, my end,

and ends

> Accept the praise I bring.

This verse gives only a few of the titles for Jesus used in the hymns of the time. Most, but not all, are individualistic. We have a wider range of names in Charles Wesley's hymn "Come, Thou Long-Expected Jesus" where he used

words that could hardly be called titles but which show
how men wanted to see Jesus:

> Hope of all the earth Thou art;
> Dear desire of every nation,
> Joy of every longing heart.

These hymn-writers seemed to be searching out new titles
to awaken in the minds of men and women a more personal and human picture of Jesus. They are titles that
usually had the authority of the Bible but which, at the same
time describe the ordinary occupations of men at that time.
They are not so much aristocratic titles describing the unique
leader, but common, democratic titles describing the occupations of many people. They were used because they
were relevant. They reflected the social conditions of the
time. They expressed the settled, middle-class life which
succeeded the civil and religious wars of the sixteenth and
seventeenth centuries. This educated, democratic, civilized life
was a new achievement. It was enjoyed indeed by a very
small proportion of the population even of Europe. But
it was the cradle of our modern world: of its science and
discovery, its philosophy and literature. It was also the soil
in which the church grew and from which it went forth in
new missionary enterprise.

These personal titles disappeared, to a great extent, from
theologcial and religious use in the next century. If it were
not that these hymns still form a substantial part of our
hymnbooks, these titles would appear strange to us. The
continuing popularity of many of these hymns indicates
that many of these titles still mean a lot to many people.

## Dare I Call Him "Mine"?

The possessive "my" still makes a strong appeal. But the hymns of the nineteenth century, especially in England, went back to older themes. They were much more medieval in tone. They tended to be otherworldly. They concentrated on death and the after life. And they recovered the military language of Christendom: "Onward, Christian Soldiers." "Fight the good fight," "The Son of God goes forth to war." In this return to the picturesque language of the past they reflected the refusal of the theologians of the time to be concerned with the immediate industrial and political situation and their ready escape into abstractions. Of course, there were movements of protest. There were the poets, the artists, and a few reformers. But the Victorian Age gave no new name to Jesus. Perhaps the Victorians did not see him as having anything to say to them.

The age of the eighteenth century hymn-writer is important for us. It reminds us that each age is called on to find its own description of Jesus; just as the next age reminds us how easy it is to disregard the call. It reminds us also that it has not been the ages of theological orthodoxy that have given us titles that have been illuminating. And we come to see that the titles that an age gives tell us perhaps as much about the age as they do about Jesus. We are left, therefore, with three questions. The first is a tempting question but one which must be rejected as irrelevant: Which of the titles that men have given Jesus in the past do we select as the most orthodox? That is not the question Jesus asks us. We can leave its answer to the scholars. The second question is inescapable: How do we in our immediate situation see Jesus today and how would we describe him? The third carries a grim warning: how far are we trying to make Jesus fit into our situation and to use him as a means to serve our ends? Or are we trying to see him belonging to this age as much as to any age in the past and with us now to rebuke, to challenge, and to inspire? For we have to see him for ourselves and to describe him in our own terms.

We are not medieval warriors defending ourselves against the attacks of Islam or going out on crusades to slaughter the infidels. We cannot today see Jesus as a warrior or a conquering hero. We can only wonder that anyone could ever have seen him as such.

We are not living the placid, settled family life of middle-class people in the villages of England or the small towns of Germany in the eighteenth century, trying to find some new meaning in their personal and domestic lives. Or if this is very much what the church is still doing, it is the reason why so many find the life of the church irrelevant in our life today. Of course many of us think of Jesus as a friend who will bring us comfort, or as an advocate who will get us off our punishment, or as a physician who will save us from all our troubles, for this is the way that we have been brought up to think of him and we cannot think of him in any other way. But we know that this is not the Jesus we see in the Gospels. And we know that our world is not the domestic settled little community in which a friend, a lawyer, and a doctor are all the help we need to meet life's personal problems. We may indeed want to escape into a quiet little world of domestic privacy, just as we find a holiday in a remote island very attractive. And it is for the same reason. We want to escape from the world of our daily work, of our contacts with all sorts of other people, and of our political responsibilities, because it is so difficult, so demanding, and so full of problems. But it is our world—the world in which we have to see Jesus if we are to see him at all.

If we are to see Jesus personally—we as persons seeing him as a person—then it is in the world to which we belong and not in the world to which we are trying to escape that we have to see him. It has always been from the world outside their comfortable lives that Jesus has come to men. This was how he came to his first disciples. They had to give up all the things to which they prefixed the adjective "my"— my home, my nets, my job, my time. They had to leave their homes, abandon their nets, and go out into the world of other men. If we are to see Jesus for ourselves with any kind of challenging reality and if we are to show him in a relevant way to other men then it is in relation to the world in which we live with other men that we have to see him and describe him.

What is this modern world like? In what way does it differ from the world of the Middle Ages—the world of Christendom, of cathedrals and crusades, of Bernard and Francis? Or from the world of the eighteenth century—the world of the Enlightenment and the French Revolution, of Wesley and Voltaire? Three things quite obviously mark our world as different: three things that were quite unknown then but are commonplace to everyone today, at least to everyone who watches TV or listens to radio anywhere. The first is that our methods of production have radically changed—from the brutish labor of the medieval field and the family economy of Wesley's England to the factory and the supermarket. The organization of industrial production has changed the pattern of the lives of men and women everywhere. It has taken them out of their homes to work, and it has changed radically the kind of life that they live in their families. Secondly, and because of this, the world knows an economic and political interdependence that is quite new. A nation's concern about its balance of payments is daily evidence of this. And thirdly there is a new realization of the urgent need to find the way to international peace through some form of world organization. This idea would have been entirely foreign to Christians in the Middle Ages and would have seemed a purposeless Utopia to men in Europe in the eighteenth century.

What has Jesus got to do with this different, modern world? How can we describe him in terms relevant to this world? It means nothing to say that he is King of kings and Lord of lords. For what have kings and lords to do with it? It means little to say that he is the redeemer, the judge, or the friend of individual men. For what is the individual's place in this modern world? We talk about this world being an impersonal world. It would be difficult to prove that it is any more impersonal than was the world of the Roman Empire or the world of Europe in the thirteenth century, at least to the majority of its people, its slaves and serfs. It would be much easier to point to the new opportunities and freedoms offered to men today. What we probably mean is that we have to adjust ourselves to new situations and learn to live with all sorts of other people in a way unknown in the past. The problem for the individual is to find how he fits into the world: to give up using the word "my" and begin to use the word "our" with as wide a connotation as possible.

How, then, can we describe Jesus? What names can we give him?

In the gospels, three names are given to Jesus which he seems to have accepted, which the church down the centuries has rarely used but which have a peculiar meaning for us today.

There is, first of all, the description that was given of Jesus as a man with a job. "Is not this the carpenter?" (Mark 6:3) This was the name that those who had known him from childhood gave him. Jesus never questioned it as an acceptable description of himself. There is a good deal about productive work in the Gospels. Just as in the Old Testament man is made in the image of God because he is called to work with God in the ordering of the world, so Jesus claims that it is in work that he is one with God: "My father goes on working and so do I." (John 5:17) Theology has never found it easy to say anything about work. The very nature of work is to be transient, changing, developing, always temporary and never finished, unending. A theology which tries to find meaning in what is abstract and unchanging can never know what to do with work—or personality. So the picture of Jesus as a worker, a producer, has never been developed in the thinking of the church. Only toward the end of last century did Jesus the carpenter appear in the paintings of some artists. Was this because men were at last becoming worried about industry? Or were they trying to escape from England's satanic mills into the lost world of the village craftsman? It is easy enough to sentimentalize Jesus as the village carpenter and to think of him as having nothing to do with modern industry. But he worked in the industry of his time as one engaged in production. Certainly if we do not see him as related to our modern industrial production we are not likely to see him as having anything really to do with our world.

It will not be easy to see him in this way. For we have never learned to think of him like this. And we will begin to do so only as we begin to think seriously about our industrial life—about the purpose of our production, the justice of its distribution, and how it can be controlled to liberate and not to enslave men. It is when we are seriously and openly concerned with these problems, and with other men, and are intent to find the way forward to a united world that we may begin to find that Jesus is speaking to us and that we understand what he is saying. We can see him as a worker and can call him a worker only as we are workers and are facing the urgent problems of our industrial world.

But the one word you cannot put before the word "worker" is "my." We cannot talk about Jesus as "my worker" as we talk about him as "my Savior" or "my Friend." We cannot be individually possessive about work. But we can talk about the world's work or God's work. This shift from "my" to "the world's" is one we have to make if we are to see Jesus in the world today.

Another title that Jesus seemed very willing to take to himself was that of servant. Obedience and reverence made his followers prefer the titles of master and lord. But we have to face the fact that "servant" was much more to his mind.

72

## Dare I Call Him "Mine"?

He did not like to be called master. He certainly did not want his disciples to be called masters or lords. The church since his day has not taken the idea of "servant" very seriously. There have, of course, been many men and women in every age who have seen their Christian obedience clearly in terms of service. And the church has always honored them. There have been orders, brotherhoods, fellowships which have seen the purpose of their corporate existence as being to serve others. But the church as a whole has been more concerned with its power, its authority, its right to instruct. And even those who serve have seen their service as being as much the service of a masterful church as of those in need. The church sees itself as a master not as a servant; servant of God, indeed, but master of the world. The church today claims that it exists to serve the world; that it is for the world. It is not very obvious to the world what this means except that the church should be to the fore in all relief enterprises. Whatever be the function of the church, it is not to serve a masterful world. And the trouble with our modern world, in all its parts, is that it is dominated by the desire to have power and to rule. The task that faces the world today is to find how we can together become a serving world. We cannot divide the world into those who serve and those who are served for, in another form, this would just be "the haves" and the "have nots." We have somehow to learn to become both served and servers. When we think of Jesus in his service of men it is in this kind of equality and mutual respect that he is seen. When we think of the task of Christians in the world today it is in this relationship to all other men that they have to live. It is not that they have to make a witness different from other people. It is rather that they have to live as citizens of the world in a way that all men have to live whoever they are.

When we begin to see Jesus as a servant we are certainly not making any claim that he is our servant. The word "my" is no more suitable before "servant" than it is before "worker." We are talking in terms of our political life. We are challenged to a complete rethinking of our economic life, or, rather, to a new thinking about it in world terms. When world bankers say that we must lend cheaply to the poor and at high rates to the rich, they are saying that service and not self-enrichment should be the policy of international finance. But it will be only when it is the policy of our family finances. John Macmurray has written recently: "The two most distinctive products of Christianity in the modern world are modern science and modern democracy" [7] It is probably only by taking science and democracy seriously that we can come to see Jesus in terms of a service, for we shall have come to see ourselves in a new way as servants of all of us. Otherwise the title is quite meaningless to us.

The third title that Jesus seemed to have been prepared to use for himself was that of "brother." He was willing to call anyone who did the will of his Father his brother and a member of his family. Presumably he called his disciples brothers. And you do not call someone your brother unless you are prepared for him to call you brother. We have seen how his disciples were reluctant to give him a title that implied their equality with him. There is no hint of their ever having called him brother. And yet he wanted to be

[7] *Theoria to Theory*, January 1969, p. 74.

seen and to be treated as on an equality with all other men. The church has followed the hesitation of the disciples. Christians have been anxious to do homage to Jesus by showing him to be as different as possible from other men. We are sinners—he was sinless. We are the sons of men—he was the Son of God. We fail—he was victorious. We hesitate to call him brother. But did he hesitate to call us brothers? Did he ever claim any status in which he was different from us? He did, indeed, do acts of healing that they seemed unable to do. But he never claimed that he alone could do them. Indeed, he assumed that they could do them, and he sent them out to heal the sick. He spoke of God with a certainty and an intimacy that surprised men. But the surprise was not so much on the note of certainty and intimacy, which is, indeed, a note quite common among religious people, as on the unexpected things he said about God. But his talk about God, which was less than we often think, never gave men the idea that he had a means of knowledge denied to them. "My Father" was always "Our Father." We have gone far astray in not always remembering that he claimed to be one of us, our brother.

We can, therefore, say "my brother." But we can do so only if we mean "our brother," the brother of all men, without distinction of race and nation, morality or creed. Our relations with other men, our equality with other men and their equality with us, be they black or white, Communist or Christian, American, Chinese, or African—this is the greatest issue that faces us in the world today. The brotherhood of man used to have a utopian ring about it. It now is the sanest of political necessities and the most difficult to realize. We dare not call Jesus brother unless we are committed to it.

The church has sometimes talked of itself as God's family. We Christians have often talked as if Jesus belonged to us in some peculiar way. We have not hesitated to apply the adjective "my" to him. We have thought of him as our possession, even though we sometimes expressed it the other way round—that we were his.

We should remember two things: The first is that the one person that Jesus never met was a Christian and one thing that he never saw was a church. If we talk, as some of us do, of our living now in a post Christian world, then we can say, with equal justice that he lived in the pre-Christian world. The men and women he talked to, the people for whom he died would not have seen any meaning in the word "Christian." This was what Paul meant when he said that "while we were yet sinners Christ died for us." If the church had not known that Jesus belonged to all men and that the family for whom he was content to die was the whole human race, they would not have gone out to the ends of the earth in his name.

The second point is that in the Gospels, Jesus in his teaching uses the word "neighbor" as much as the word "brother," and with a more positive meaning. For him the neighbor was not just the person next door. It was his name for everyone else: including those who belonged to wider and even hostile groups, such as the Samaritans. There was no limit to those who were a man's neighbors. This was new teaching. Also new was his teaching on how one treated ones neighbors. Men were to love their neighbors. This, of course, was part of the old law. What was new was Jesus' interpretation of the law to include loving your enemies.

In the Epistles fellow-Christian takes the place of neighbor. "Love of the brethren" takes priority over love of all men. One can appreciate from Paul's letters how overriding were the problems of building up a new community life among those who declared themselves Christians. But something very serious happened to the mission of the church when the fellow-Christian took the place of the universal neighbor as the object of the church's concern. This internal concern has remained to a very great extent the emphasis of the church and is now the greatest obstacle to the advance of the mission of Christ in the world today. This was not so obvious in the past when the agents of the church's mission were the appointed and paid servants of the church—the monks of the Dark Ages, the missionary societies of the last two centuries, and at all times the ordained ministry. Now that the mission of the church is no longer to other lands but to our new one world, the work cannot be carried out by deputies—by men and women sent out and paid to do it—but by Christians everywhere in their own secular jobs and in their ordinary political responsibilities. This radical change in the area and manner of the church's mission will be made only as we see Jesus as belonging not to the church but to all men, as Paul and his contemporaries saw clearly.

Because of its concern with its own life, the church has never trained its members to work with other people. Indeed, the concern of the church-member has been so much with the life of the church in its smaller units—the congregation or the denomination—that the church now feels that it has

77

achieved something noteworthy when in recent decades it
has persuaded members of differing denominations to work
together on some issues. Christians are still very hesitant to
work on common objects with those of other beliefs, religious
or political. But when we call Jesus "brother," we are committed to treat all other men as brothers. He is the brother
of all men. And if all other men do not see him as their
brother—or do not see him at all—it is because we have made
him our possession. They can indeed see him only in other
men and if we are the men in whom alone they can see him
they are not always attracted by what they see. Our knowledge of Jesus is the key we hold which opens doors for
others or keeps them shut. We lock people out by the dis-
torted picture we offer of Jesus. They can also, of course,
lock themselves out by their dislike of the true picture,
if they see it.

In Swinburne's verses:

Thou hast conquered, O pale Galilean;
    the world has grown gray from thy breath;[8]

Swinburne was not thinking only of the dullness of life in
late Victorian England. He was quoting from Ibsen's huge
twofold drama *Emperor and Galilean* which tells, with
sympathy, of the Emperor Julian's attempt to overthrow
Christianity and restore the old religion of Rome and of his
failure. At the end of the play Julian falls back crying:
"Thou hast conquered, Galilean." [9]

[8] Algernon Charles Swinburne, *Hymn to Proserpine*.
[9] Henrick Ibsen, *League of Youth and Emperor and Galilean*, James
McFarlane, trans. (Oxford University Press, 1963), p. 467.

## Dare I Call Him "Mine"?

Ibsen and Swinburne saw that something, as they saw it, of freedom and joy had been lost to the world, but they had no doubt that Jesus had conquered, and the world would never be the same again: the world was now his though they did not like what they saw. Their dislike is expressed in their use of the name Galilean for Jesus. It expresses for them what is parochial, unsophisticated, unimportant. For Ibsen there is still the abiding mystery of its power, as expressed in part of the final main speech of Julian:

Then I looked down on my own earth—the Emperor's earth, which I had made Galileanless—and I thought that all that I had done was very good.

But behold, my Maximus,—there came a procession by me, on the strange earth where I stood. There were soldiers, and judges, and executioners at the head of it, and weeping women followed. And lo—in the midst of the slow-moving array, was the Galilean, alive, and bearing a cross on his back. Then I called to him, and said, "Whither away, Galilean?" But he turned his face toward me, smiled, nodded slowly and said: "To the place of the skull." Where is he now? What if that at Golgotha, near Jerusalem, was but a wayside matter, a thing done, as it were in the passing, in a leisure hour? What if he goes on and on, and suffers, and dies, and conquers, from world to world?

Oh that I could lay waste the world.[10]

Ibsen would not have used the word "pale" to describe the Galilean. There was nothing pale in the Christians with whom Julian had to contend. Much as he disliked their faith, Julian contrasts the cold admiration the Greeks and Romans had for their heroes with "the Galilean, the car-

<hr>

[10] *Emperor and Galilean*, p. 456.

penter's son, who sits as the king of love in the warm, believing hearts of men." [11] But Swinburne saw the world as having grown grey and Jesus as a pallid figure. And if he did, whose was the responsibility? We can dismiss him as a superficial dilettante. But we cannot dismiss so easily the failure of the church to show Jesus otherwise.

We fail to show Jesus to men when we keep him as our possession. Whenever we apply the word "my" to him, we show to men that our interest is really in ourselves.

Alfred Whitehead, the philosopher, has redeemed the word "Galilean" for us. He sees it as a significant description of Jesus. He speaks of "the brief Galilean vision of humility as the light that flickers throughout the ages." [12] If we are to see Jesus for ourselves and be able in any way to show him to other men, then perhaps we have to learn a little of Galilean humility. We could begin by abolishing "my" from our vocabulary when speaking about Jesus and talk of him as "ours" or "the world's." We find it difficult to share him with other men. But we can only dare to say that Jesus died for me if we believe that he died in the first place for other men. In the same way we hesitate to call him "Worker," "Servant," and "Brother" because we are afraid of what would be demanded of us if we were to be workers, servants, and brothers with all other men. We much prefer to see ourselves as consumers, as those who show others that we can use the world's resources temperately for ourselves and give a little that is over to them; as those who are entitled to instruct others, with courtesy, of course,

---

[11] *Ibid.*, p. 455.
[12] Alfred North Whitehead, *Process and Reality* (New York: Macmillan, 1967), p. 520.

but also with the authority of superior knowledge; as those who will welcome others into our family, on conditions.

A moral, intellectual, and ecclesiastical revolution is demanded of us if we are to give these names to Jesus—worker, servant, brother.

# How Do Men See Him Today?

"This is a difficult country, and our home."

Edwin Muir

How do we see Jesus today? How would we recognize his presence in our world now? How do we see him belonging to this difficult world which is our home? For if we do not see him as in some way belonging to it, we will not be able to see him at all.

How would we recognize him? Down the centuries there must have been more pictures drawn of Jesus than of any other man. And yet we do not know what he looked like. We have been given no ready sign by which we should recognize him. The four Gospels give us no description of him: neither of his height nor of his weight, neither of the color of his eyes nor of his hair, neither of the expression of his face nor of the tone of his voice. All that we know is that he was a man and looked an ordinary man. Malta treasures what it claims to be the oldest picture of Jesus. It is the drawing of the face of Jesus which the people claim was made by Luke during the long winter of waiting after he and Paul and the others were shipwrecked on their way to Rome. We can well believe that Luke talked a lot about Jesus for he had been gathering information in Palestine about his childhood and ministry for the writing of his Gospel. It is also highly probable that he drew pictures to give point to what he was saying, for Luke was obviously a bit of an artist. But it is highly improbable that the picture Malta treasures is the one he drew. The original drawing may well have been retraced and copied many times but still bearing his name as the artist. But all that it tells us is that Jesus was a man with eyes and mouth and nose like other men. And this indeed was the point that Luke was making: that he was talking about a man; a man who looked like any other man; a man who was born in a stable and taught and healed and died on a cross; a man of their own time.

Of course we think we know what Jesus looked like. We think we would recognize him if he came into our house or walked along our street. But the only way in which he could conform to our picture of him would be that he would not look a man of our time. For the picture we have of him in our minds is the composite memory of those we have seen drawn by the artists of other centuries. And they saw him as belonging to their time and so they dressed him in the clothes and against the background of the life of their time. And those today who have to represent Jesus in school textbooks, in Sunday school outlines, in evangelical posters, and in many of the windows of our churches copy this old tradition. If they followed the example of the artists themselves and showed Jesus as a man of our time no one would recognize him. But we know that the copy-book figure must be Jesus because it could not be anyone else. Of one thing we can be certain, and this is that Jesus looked nothing like our picture of him. The only ones of this kind of propaganda cartoon which impress with any sense of reality and vitality are those which show him in a setting he never knew and wearing clothes he never wore and with the features of another race, as, for instance, the pictures of Chinese and African artists. They draw him as a contemporary, and he is recognizable.

All who have painted lively pictures of Jesus have drawn on their imagination and not on any information. We owe a great deal to those artists of the past. They have helped millions of people to see Jesus as a man who lived on earth, an individual person. For the artist has to be particular. He cannot generalize. He may draw many different pictures of the one person but each one will be particular, with its peculiar expression, posture, and impression. None may be the least adequate. But there can never be any doubt that the artist is depicting one individual person. He can never do what those who use words—the theologian and the preacher—can do; he can never say, "He may be like this," or "He may be like that," and leave his hearers with the impression that he is dealing with an idea and not a person. This may be the reason why Catholic churches, which have depended on pictures rather than on words, have, despite the lack of education of their people and the rigidity of their theology, often in the past given a more human picture of Jesus than have the Protestant churches, which, despite the better education of their people and the Bible put in their hands to read, have left them with the impression that the object of their belief was a dogma rather than a person. In all churches it is the artist, including the popularizer and the hymn-writer, who has given people their picture of Jesus. And we owe them a great debt.

But the cost that we have paid is that the picture is always out of date. It belongs to another age. Jesus is, therefore, thought of as belonging to the past, as clothed in fancy dress. The artists who have given us this picture did not see him in this way. They did not think of him as belonging to another age or as dressed in strange clothes. They painted him as a man of their own time. They saw him as belonging to their world, as speaking to them in it, as interpreting their own life to them. They saw him as in a real sense their representative, sharing and interpreting their situation, their suffering, their hopes. So it is always as a man that they paint him, suffering or triumphant, humiliated or glorious; but never a superman, always a man. And, because they have to paint him in particularity, they paint him as they saw him—as a contemporary.

But, of course, it has not been quite so simple as this sounds. Other factors have influenced the artist in addition to his intention of drawing Jesus as a man. He is affected by the artistic tradition he has inherited. He is dependent on the impression of Jesus he has received from others. The church has generally let it be known that its first demand on art is that it should instruct. It has wanted to use art to expound doctrine. In the early centuries, and especially in the Eastern church, the artist had to withstand the church's fear of images. "Anthropomorphic art ultimately emerged victorious but it had to struggle constantly against the hostile attitude of the iconoclasts who denied that Divinity could be depicted . . . the anthropomorphic image underwent a systematic revision in the direction of ever greater abstraction." [1]

We see these forces at play in the early pictures of Jesus. The pictures of Jesus in the catacombs show him young and beardless. When the church was recognized by the Empire and Christians were free to worship in public and above ground, the picture changed. "The very youthful Christ disappeared almost with the adoption of Christianity as the official religion." [2] On the ceiling of the apse of their new basilican churches they set in mosaic for all to see the picture of the triumphant Christ, ruling not only in the hearts of his followers but ruling the Roman world, the Galilean who had conquered, wearing the symbols not of his suffering but of his rule. This was the picture that the church wanted all men to see. But this picture of the triumphant Christ, risen, ascended, did not remain static. It was changed to

[1] D. Talbot Rice, *Encyclopedia of World Art*, II (New York: McGraw-Hill, 1960), 769.

[2] D. Talbot Rice, *The Beginnings of Christian Art* (Nashville: Abingdon Press, 1958), p. 66.

fit a later age. Professor Talbot Rice describes a later mosaic thus:

The Christ is a massive impressive, ageless figure, with long black hair and in a thick black beard, who stands poised in space with His arm raised in blessing; the background, with its flame-coloured clouds, seems to extend into limitless space behind. . . . Here we see for the first time in art an expression of the esoteric, transcendental faith which was now becoming an essential feature of Christianity, based not so much on the teaching of Christ Himself as on the ideas that had penetrated from the East, together with the arguments and teaching of the Fathers of the Church.[3]

Christendom of the Middle Ages showed men a very different picture, especially in its later centuries. Then the constant picture shown was that of Jesus on the cross, with eyes closed in death and blood dripping from his wounds. It was a picture usually carved in stone or wood, as if wrought out of the very material of Europe's endurance and suffering. It was displayed to men not only in every cathedral and parish church but in every wayside shrine and carried on men's bodies: the symbol of human suffering and endurance and of individual piety.

These pictures, of the triumphant and of the suffering Christ, are still with us. But they have not given us our conventional picture of Jesus. We are heirs of the Renaissance in this as in so much else. Our unthinking picture of Jesus is that painted by the artists of the fifteenth, sixteenth, and seventeenth centuries, particularly in Italy and the

[3] *Ibid.*, p. 69.

Netherlands. They painted life as they saw it in the wonder of their discovery of the material world, in their love of the beauty of the human body, and in their trust in the nobility and power of the mind of man. There was nothing that they dared not paint—from the gods and goddesses of the ancient world to the horrors of Hell and the joys of Heaven. But it was man's life that was their chosen subject and the man they painted with most interest was Jesus. This was not just because the church was the great patron of the arts, for the church's choice ranged far wider than the gospel. It was rather that in Jesus they saw man in all the range of life from birth through manhood to death and after and in all the width of human emotion in relationship with other men—family, friends, enemies, the sick, the greedy, the crowd. They painted life as they saw it when they painted him. They saw Jesus as the man of their time, human in his suffering, victorious in the power of his tenderness, holding the key to the mystery of life.

Since then have men painted any new picture of Jesus? Artists have made pictures of him in plenty; in paint, in glass, in wood, or in stone. They have either reproduced the Renaissance picture or they have attempted a new historical accuracy; trying to reconstruct the carpenter's shop in Nazareth or the vegetation of the wilderness. Why is this? We have not dared to paint him in contemporary dress or against a modern background. Is it because we do not know where we would set him? In the village or in the city? And if the city, East end or West end? And which city? Moscow or Washington, London or Peking? And whose dress would he wear? A motor-mechanic's or a peasant's?

## How Do Men See Him Today?

A clergyman's or a policeman's? It is safer to keep him a conventional figure in fancy dress and to identify him by a halo, or a crown of thorns, a beard or a sickly smile.

Our fundamental difficulty is that we do not know what man should look like today. The ages that could draw a picture that all recognized as being of Jesus did so because they knew what a man should look like. If we are in difficulties it is not because we are not studying and discussing man and trying to understand the meaning of man's life today. It is rather because we see so much that is baffling and new. When we think of man today we are not thinking as men thought in the first Christian centuries of man in a self-contained world—the world of the Roman Empire. Nor are we thinking, as the men of the Renaissance did, of Europe awakening to new possibilities of power and discovery. Today when we think of man we have to think of all men—black and white and yellow; Asian, African, European, American. We have to think of man in quite a new way. We have not even yet got a word to describe him: universal, international, ecumenical? All are questioned and inadequate. And yet we must find some simple word to describe a man as a fellow of all other men, a citizen of the world. And man today has power and opportunity unknown before. And because of this he is aware of himself in a new way, with doubts and desires, hopes and fears unknown before. It would indeed be surprising if any older picture of Jesus fitted into this new world. Men today will not see Jesus for themselves until they begin to see themselves more clearly; unless they begin to see themselves in Jesus.

## Jesus: Man for Today

It may be that our inability to depict Jesus in contemporary dress and our refusal to be satisfied any longer with fancy dress indicate that something else is first required of us. It may be that we are now so accustomed to getting our news through our eyes and judging things by our first seeing of them that we cannot penetrate in thought behind what we see. Perhaps line and color have become too much means of reporting. Perhaps we are finding it more difficult to express ideas through them. It may be that words are becoming again the main means by which we express ideas and draw our picture of Jesus. This, of course, was where it all began. When those who had seen Jesus wanted to show Jesus to those who had not they wrote the Gospels. We should be forever grateful that they were not illustrated, as they would have been today. Words by themselves make a demand on the reader's or hearer's response. If he receives them he has, in some way, to interpret them. The gospels do not tell us what Jesus looked like. They tell us of his mind and of his actions. They tell us what kind of man he was. But only if we ask some questions.

So today we should not perhaps be surprised that we turn, not to the artists, but to the poets and to the dramatists and even to the philosophers for our picture of Jesus as men see him today. Their task it is to try to see and describe man's life today and for this reason many of them give direct or indirect pictures of Jesus. It would be a daunting enterprise to try to assess all that the poets, dramatists, and philosophers have to say about man today and as impossible to distill their references to Jesus. Rather than make inadequately founded generalizations it seems better to take one poet in particular and to try to understand how he sees Jesus today. No great poet is typical any more than a great painter is typical. By nature of his calling he has some unique quality. But any poet must reflect and interpret the experience of other men and the greater he is the more fully he does it.

The chosen poet is Edwin Muir. He is chosen because through all his life and in all his writings he was concerned with the meaning of man's life on earth, in the past and in the present. "He was interested in his own life in the same way as he might have been in the life of another if he could have known it as well, not because it was his own but as a means of penetrating to some understanding of the meaning of human life in general." [4] As he wrote in his diary: "The Eternal Man has possessed me during most of the time that I have been writing my Autobiography, and has possessed me in most of my poetry." And for him this understanding of man and of his life came to center more and more on Jesus. In a letter to a fellow poet he wrote: "'I believe in God, in the immortality of the soul, and that Christ is the greatest figure who ever appeared in the history of mankind. I believe in the Fall too, and the need of salvation. But theological dogmas do not help me; I can't digest them for my good; they're an obstacle to me (perhaps they shouldn't be, but they are); and so I'm a sort of illicit Christian, a gate-crasher, hoping in my own way to slip in 'At David's hip yet.'" [5] In this he is not unrepresentative of many men and women today.

[4] Peter T. Butter, *Edwin Muir: Man and Poet* (New York: Barnes & Noble, 1966), p. 170.
[5] *Ibid.*, p. 183.

Edwin Muir was born in 1887 in the Orkneys and spent his childhood there. He began his working life in ill-paid clerical jobs in industry in Glasgow and Greenock. He later served the British Council as their representative in Prague and Rome. He was then appointed as Warden of Newbattle Abbey, near Edinburgh, Scotland's one residential college of adult education. He was author of many works in prose and verse and Professor of Poetry at Harvard. He died in Cambridge, England, in 1959.

No man is typical. But Edwin Muir can be said to represent much of the experience of European man in the first half of the twentieth century. His roots were in a self-contained and self-supporting community of farmers and fisherman. As a young man he knew through personal experience the pains and frustrations of industrial depression and the squalor of life for the poor in Glasgow before the first World War. From long residence in Europe, on both sides of the iron curtain, and as translator with his wife, Willa Muir, of Kafka, Feuchtwanger, and other European writers he knew the despair of a war-broken continent. Involved for most of his life in international contacts and in adult education, he could never escape from the clash of hope and despair.

And yet what he sees is not what everyone else sees. But what he sees we recognize with surprise as being in our field of vision. And so he helps us to know ourselves and to know something of our history and present predicament.

It is a very personal view of the world that we find expressed in his early poetry. It is the intense vision of a child brought up on a remote island with very little to distract his seeing. It is probably a view common to most children, at least intermittently. But for Muir it was intense, constant and formative. He spent his childhood on a farm in Orkney with, above him, the beauty of wide skies and, around him, the austerity of stormy seas and treeless fields; in a close-knit community of family and neighbors with his imagination formed by the reading of the Bible in his happy but not particularly religious home and by the hearing of the folktales of an island and seafaring people. His was an intense and never questioned sense of the natural life around him of which he was part. He called the first version of his autobiography, which dealt mainly with his earlier years, *The Story and the Fable*, because he was so acutely aware of the intertwining of his own life and of the interpretation of all life. In it he writes: "There are times in every man's life when he seems to become for a little while a part of the fable, and to be recapitulating some legendary dream which, as it has recurred a countless number of times in time, is ageless. The realization of the Fall is one of these evants, and the purifications which happen in one's life belong to them too. The realization of the Fall is a realization of a universal event: and the two purifications which I have described, the one in Kirkwall and the other in Glasgow, brought with them images of universal purification. After the night in Kirkwall I felt that not only myself but every one was saved, or would some time be saved: and my conversion to socialism somehow had a similar effect. It was as if I had stepped into a fable that was always there, invisibly waiting for any one who wished to enter it." [6]

[6] Edwin Muir, *The Story and the Fable* (London: Harrap, 1940), p. 134.

# Jesus: Man for Today

The Fall, the Incarnation, and Eden are in the background of most of his poetry and often in the titles of his poems, especially Eden. But these biblical themes are not seen to belong to the past or to be interpreted as principles or abstractions but as illustrating the present. The "Story" and the "Fable" become one. They are talking about the same things. The story is what we live. The fable is what we hear. And life is one. This linking of the present and the past is strong in his early poems.

> We through the generations come
> Here by a way we do not know
> From the fields of Abraham,
> And still the road is scarce begun.[7]

> Yet we the latest born are still
> The first one and the last,
> And in our little measures fill
> The oceanic past.[8]

So past is present now. Fable and story intertwine. Eden is never far distant. Eden seems sometimes to be the Orkney of his childhood and yet

> One foot in Eden still, I stand
> and look across the other land.[9]

In his *Autobiography* Muir describes how in a very simple and natural way he, in 1939, suddenly realized that he was a Christian. "I had believed for many years in God. . . . My

[7] Edwin Muir, "The Succession," in *Collected Poems*, p. 221.
[8] "Twice-Done, Once-Done" in *Collected Poems*, p. 135.
[9] "One Foot in Eden" in *Collected Poems*, p. 227.

belief receded then, it is true, to an unimaginable distance, but it still stood there, not in any territory of mine, it seemed, but in a place of its own. Now I realized that, quite without knowing it, I was a Christian, no matter how bad a one; and I remembered a few days later that Janet Adam Smith had told me, half-teasingly, while I was staying in Hampstead, that my poetry was Christian poetry; the idea then had been quite strange to me. I had a vague sense during these days that Christ was the turning point of time and the meaning of life to everyone, no matter what his conscious beliefs; to my agnostic friends as well as Christians. I read the New Testament many times during the following months, particularly the Gospels. I did not turn to any Church, and my talks with ministers and divines cast me back on the Gospels again, which was probably the best thing that could have happened." [10]

Jesus had stepped from the fable into the story of his life. But it was only then in later life that he saw him as a real person. He says this of his upbringing in the church in Orkney: "During the time when, as a boy, I attended the United Presbyterian Church in Orkney, I was aware of religion chiefly as the sacred Word, and the church itself, severe and decent, with its touching bareness and austerity, seemed to cut off religion from the rest of life and from all the week-day world, as if it were a quite specific thing shut within itself, almost jealously, by its white-washed walls, furnished with its bare brown varnished benches unlike any others in the whole world, and filled with the odour of

[10] Edwin Muir, *An Autobiography* (New York: Seabury Press, 1968), p. 247.

ancient Bibles. Instead there was the minister." And he goes
on to tell of two: one greatly loved and the other greatly
admired. "In figures such as these the Word became something more than a word in my childish mind; but nothing
told me that Christ was born in the flesh and had lived on
earth." [11] It is hard for us to realize how true this was of the
church of last century. We find it hard to accept how little
the person and teaching of Jesus entered into the preaching
and teaching of the church. Muir's experience was noteworthy only in that he came to see Jesus as a man who had
lived on earth. His story should remind us of our debt to the
liberals who rediscovered the life of Christ and wrote about
the Jesus of History. It should also remind us how slowly
new views percolate down into the ordinary life and thinking
of the church.

Muir goes on in his *Autobiography* to explain how it was
only later, in Rome, that the meaning of Jesus' life on earth
was borne in on him. He tells how the image of Jesus was to
be seen everywhere "not only in churches, but on the walls
of houses, at crossroads in the suburbs, in wayside shrines in
the parks, and in private rooms. I remember stopping for a
long time one day to look at a little plaque on the wall of
a house in the Via degli Artisti, representing the Annuncia-
tion. An angel and a young girl, their bodies inclined
towards each other, their knees bent as if they were overcome
by love, 'tutto tremante', gazed upon each other like
Dante's pair; and that representation of human love so intense that it could not reach further seemed the perfect
earthly symbol of the love that passes understanding. A

[11] *Ibid.*, p. 277.

religion that dared to show forth such a mystery for everyone to see would have shocked the congregations of the north, would have seemed a sort of blasphemy, perhaps even an indecency. But here it was publicly shown, as Christ showed himself on earth." [12]

The first effect of his realization that he was a Christian was that prayer became real to him, especially the Lord's Prayer. Indeed it was through finding himself repeating the Lord's Prayer that he woke up to the fact that he was a Christian. "I never realized before so clearly the primary importance of 'we' and 'us' in the prayer: it is collective, for all societies, for all mankind as a great society. . . .The difference here between 'I' and 'we' is tremendous: there is no end to the conclusions that follow from it. In 'we' it is man, or mankind, or the community, or all the communities, that is speaking: it is human life, and therefore society is the formal embodiment of human life. And to pray as 'we' is not only to embrace in the prayer all human life, all the aspirations of mankind for the perfect kingdom when God's will shall be done on earth; it is for the individual soul a pledge for all other souls, an act of responsibility, and an act of union which strengthens him from within and at the same time lends him infinite strength from without. Yet how many centuries this prayer has been recited as if it were the multiplication table." [13]

But he was not led to identify himself with the church. Indeed the church seemed to represent all the things that had prevented him from seeing Jesus sooner. He wrote in his

[12] *Ibid.*, p. 278.
[13] P. T. Butter, *Edwin Muir: Man and Poet*, pp. 168-69.

diary: "Walking to the pier (at St. Andrews) yesterday, I seemed to see that a Church which is not universal and all-inclusive is evil by virtue of that fact alone for it rejects mankind. All Churches which do this are fond of the doctrine of Hell and consign great multitudes to damnation." [14] His anger with the church was not only because it divided men. It was rather that it had made Jesus an abstraction and "God three angry letters in a book." The poem continues:

> And there the logical hook
> On which the Mystery is impaled and bent
> Into an ideological instrument.
> There's better gospel in man's natural tongue,
> And truer sight was theirs outside the Law
> Who saw the far side of the Cross among
> The archaic people in their ancient awe,
> In ignorant wonder saw
> The wooden cross-tree on the bare hillside,
> Not knowing that there a God suffered and died.

He goes on to show how we are afraid of life and escape into abstractions:

> The fleshless word, growing, will bring us down,
> Pagan and Christian man alike will fall,
> The Auguries say, the white and black and brown,
> The merry and sad, theorist, lover, all
> Invisibly will fall:
> Abstract calamity, save for those who can
> Build their cold empire on the abstract man. [15]

[14] Edwin Muir, *The Story and the Fable*, p. 256.
[15] "The Incarnate One" in *Collected Poems*, p. 228.

## How Do Men See Him Today?

But how does he see Jesus?

He saw him, firstly, as one who was "born in the flesh and had lived on earth." With vivid eyes he saw, as many others see today, the life he lived of open identification with all other men, and, because of it, of suffering. On this openness to all men, he writes in words put into the mouth of the disciples:

> And when we went into the town, he with us,
> The lurkers under doorways, murderers,
> With rags tied round their feet for silence, came
> Out of themselves to us and were with us,
> And those who hide within the labyrinth
> Of their own loneliness and greatness came,
> And those entangled in their own devices,
> The silent and the garrulous liars, all
> Stepped out of their dungeons and were free.[16]

In another poem in words put into the mouth of a stranger in Jerusalem he describes the death of Jesus:

> We watched the writhings, heard the moanings, saw
> The three heads turning on their separate axles
> Like broken wheels left spinning. Round his head
> Was loosely bound a crown of plaited thorn
> That hurt at random, stinging temple and brow
> As the pain swung into its envious circle.
> . . . Some
> Who came to stare grew silent as they looked,
> Indignant or sorry. But the hardened old

[16] "The Transfiguration" in *Collected Poems,* p. 199.

And the hard-hearted young, although at odds
From the first morning, cursed him with one curse,
Having prayed for a Rabbi or an armed Messiah
And found the Son of God . . .
The Sun revolved, the shadow wheeled,
The evening fell. His head lay on his breast,
But in his breast they watched his heart move on
By itself alone, accomplishing its journey.
Their taunts grew louder, sharpened by the knowledge
That he was walking in the park of death,
Far from their rage. Yet all grew stale at last,
Spite, curiosity, envy, hate itself.
They waited only for death and death was slow
And came so quietly they scarce could mark it.
They were angry then with death and death's deceit.[17]

Muir sees Jesus as he lived and taught and suffered and
died in Palestine. He does not see him with any particular
Palestinian or Jewish background. He sees him rather as a
man living in the world of other men.

Edwin Muir's intense sense of the intimacy, wonder, and
mystery of the natural world, which was so evident in his
childhood and lasted on through all his life, must have been
not unlike the awareness of Jesus that this was his Father's
world, who knew that heaven was open to men on earth and
that God spoke to men on earth. This may be why Muir
saw Jesus in a peculiar relationship to the things of the earth
and therefore to the past and to the future. He sees Jesus
not just as one who lived his life on earth but as one who is
still in all life.

[17] "The Killing" in Collected Poems, p. 225.

## How Do Men See Him Today?

It's said that to reverse its doom
    And save the entangled Soul, to earth
God came and entered in the womb
    And passed through the gate of birth;

Was born a Child in body bound
    Among the cattle in a byre.
The clamourous world was all around,
    Beast, insect, plant, earth, water, fire.

On bread and wine his flesh grew tall,
    The round sun helped him on his way,
Wood, iron, herb and animal
    His friends were till the testing day.

Then braced by iron and by wood,
    Engrafted on a tree he died,
And little dogs lapped up the blood
    That spurted from his broken side.

.    .    .    .    .    .    .

There all at last with all was done,
    The great knot loosened, flesh unmade
Beyond the kingdom of the sun,
    In the invincible shade.

All that had waited for his birth
    Were round him then in dusty night,
The creatures of the swarming earth,
    The souls and angels in the height.[18]

Muir sees Jesus as belonging to all men, bad and good alike. He sees him also as identified with the material world, not only in its beauty but also in its cruelty and suffering. There is nothing sentimental or romantic in his view of the

---

[18] "Thought and Image" in *Collected Poems*, pp. 133-34.

world. So, though he goes back in thought to Eden, sometimes seemingly identified with the Orkney of his childhood, it is with the present that he is concerned and in which Jesus lives.

> But famished field and blackened tree
> Bear flowers in Eden never known.
> Blossoms of grief and charity
> Bloom in these darkened fields alone.
> What had Eden ever to say
> Of hope and faith and pity and love
> Until was buried all its day
> And memory found its treasure trove?
> Strange blessings never in Paradise
> Fall from these beclouded skies.[19]

This certainty of purpose in the present leads him to look to the future. And the future for him is Christ.

> But he will come again, it's said, though not
> Unwanted and unsummoned; for all things,
> Beasts of the fields, and woods, and rocks, and seas,
> And all mankind from end to end of the earth
> Will call him with one voice. In our own time,
> Some say, or at a time when time is ripe.
> Then he will come, Christ the uncrucified,
> Christ the discrucified, his death undone,
> His agony unmade, his cross dismantled—
> Glad to be so—and the tormented wood
> Will cure its hurt and grow into a tree
> In a green springing corner of young Eden,
> And Judas damned take his long journey backward

[19] "One Foot in Eden" in *Collected Poems*, p. 227.

From darkness into light and be a child
Beside his mother's knee, and the betrayal
Be quite undone and never more be done.[20]

This is not the church's conventional picture of the Second Coming or of the Last Things. That picture is so strange that most Christians today shy away from it. And yet the physical future hurries to meet us with a terrifying speed. Muir's vision is intelligible. His picture of all things being restored to their original purpose expresses in concrete terms Paul's general vision of the consummation of all things in Christ. And when has forgiveness been so universally and so deeply expressed as in the picture of Judas forgiven and restored?

As he was dying, Edwin Muir said urgently to his wife: "There are no absolutes, no absolutes." His poetry and his life express his fear of all abstractions, of men's attempts to reduce life to absolutes. He saw them as the enemies of life. Where people are there is life. And where life is there are no absolutes. For Muir the key of life was in the Eternal Man, Jesus. This seems to be the message of his poetry.

We have taken some time to see what one modern poet has to say about Jesus. We must be careful not to read too much into our understanding of his poetry. We must realize that he is not typical. But we must take his picture with far more seriousness than we give to the medieval or Renaissance pictures that we have inherited, for it is contemporary. It comes out of this difficult country which is our home. And Edwin Muir was not thinking of Scotland.

[20] "The Transfiguration" in *Collected Poems*, p. 200.

He was thinking of the world, whatever our country be, this universal human society that is now our home. He shows us where we have to see Jesus now if we are to see him at all: in the open life he lived with all men in Palestine, in his presence now as the key of all life—the life of the world, not just the life of the church, and in God's purpose for the world to which we commit ourselves.[21]

[21] For further information on Edwin Muir, see:
Muir, *Collected Poems* (Oxford University Press)
   *The Story and the Fable: An Autobiography* (Harrap)
   *An Autobiography* (Seabury Press)
   *Literature and Society* (Hogarth Press)
Willa Muir, *Belonging: A Memoir* (Hogarth Press)
P. T. Butter, *Edwin Muir: Man and Poet* (Barnes & Noble)
Donald Mathers, "Edwin Muir and the Incarnation," in *The Church and the Modern World* (Ryerson Press)

# Free to Believe

In the last three chapters we have discussed three lines of approach in the business of finding some adequate name to describe Jesus today. Perhaps it has seemed as if these chapters were meant to be a historical survey of the titles given to Jesus during the course of the church's history. If this were indeed so, many gaps would be obvious. But this was not the intention. The purpose was rather to discuss the different ways in which men have seen Jesus and tried to describe him. We recognized three ways which are distinct in themselves and yet never entirely separate. Each way finds particular emphasis at certain times in the church's history.

First we saw how the people of the early church were peculiarly concerned with the place of Jesus in the world in which they lived, both the political world and the natural world. This was inevitable because their knowledge of him was of a life that had been lived in their world of space and time. Personal devotion was taken for granted. The questions they asked and other men asked were about the place of Jesus in the world of men and of nature. The title they gave him of "Lord" expressed his supreme position there. This was their interest. It is one which we today cannot avoid discussing.

In the next chapter we considered the names which men gave to Jesus when they had emerged from the religious wars and the theological disputes of the middle ages and the Reformation and had settled down to a more peaceful life of commerce and domesticity and to a wider world of knowledge and exploration. They were not so much concerned with the place of Jesus in nature as with their own personal response to him in piety and worship. And this, of course, is a constant element of faith.

In the last chapter we considered a way of portraying Jesus which has been present in all ages but which takes a different form in each age: the use of art to show Jesus in visible form or in words, as an expression of faith or as an aid to devotion or for propaganda. We saw how today the artist's contribution is more likely to be made with vivid impact in words rather than in line and color. But the way of the artist is always with us.

We could give a variety of names to these three lines of approach. We could say that they are concerned respectively with the place of Jesus in the world in which we live, with his place in the interior world of our experience and devotion, and with him as the subject of our artistic expression. We could call them the approaches through the mind, the will and the imagination. Or, we could see them as the approaches through faith or love or hope. In a more limited way we could talk of the approach of the scientist, the religious man, and the artist. But however we express them and however clearly we emphasize the peculiar differences between them, we should remember that each has had its place with the other two in the picture of Jesus that each age has given to us. And each has its place in the mental picture which each one of us has of Jesus today. Our picture of Jesus, if it is to be at all adequate, must see him set in the world of our ordinary experience. It must evoke a willing and loving response in us. And it must stir our imagination so that what we see can be interpreted in a living and visible way to others. In each one of us, and at particular times, one of these approaches may well predominate. But these three will always be there, different but intermingled, in the thoughts of each of us and in the life of the church.

But are these three the only lines of approach? It may seem to some that the most important line of approach has been omitted. Science, devotion, and art have been mentioned. But where is theology? Surely it is to the theologians that we turn when we want to know what to call Jesus rather than to the scientists, the religious, and the artists. More specifically, there are the names given to him in the creeds, and echoed in the prayers and worship of the church. The Apostles' Creed calls him God's "only Son our Lord." The Nicene Creed proclaims "one Lord Jesus Christ, the only begotten Son of God, Begotten of His Father before all worlds, God of God, Light of Light, Very God of Very God, Begotten not made, being of one substance with the Father, by whom all things were made . . ." Is not this the name we give him, the only name that matters—"Son of God"?

Why has this name been omitted? There are several reasons. The first is that these words do not help men today to see Jesus. An education in scholastic theology is needed to explain them and, when explained, they leave our questions about Jesus still unanswered.

Then these words of the Creeds could never be said to be the ways in which men have ever described Jesus to themselves or to others. Instead they have used pictures and stories and signs and titles. For you can describe someone to others only in pictures or words that they can understand. So the first Christians called him just "Jesus" or "Jesus whom you crucified" or "Jesus who went about doing good." And then, as they moved out from Jerusalem, they called him "Lord"; and later "King," "Conqueror"; and, much later still, "Shepherd, Husband, Friend." They were using familiar names that their contemporaries understood to help them to understand what Jesus was like. When the church called Jesus "Son of God," it was not trying to give Jesus a descriptive name. Perhaps in the beginning it was trying to reflect something of Jesus' own teaching about God and his attitude to God but soon it became something very different and very difficult to explain to those outside the church. It has not been from this phrase that men's picture of Jesus has ever come. Indeed it has blurred the clearness of the picture that men can have of Jesus. It is elsewhere than to theological statements that men have looked for illumination. The Gospels rather than the Epistles give us our picture of Jesus. The picture that men have of Jesus has come from the report of his actions and his words in the gospels, from other men's attempts to reflect him in their own lives, from the ways in which men have tried to reveal him in words spoken in sermon or acted in drama or uttered in conversation and expressed in painting, carving, and poetry. These are the ways in which men see a picture of Jesus. Theology, in the more formal sense in which we use the word today, has a different task.

Theology means our thinking about our whole experience of God. We have to be careful how we use the word. Men can have deep thoughts about God without using any other language than the words of everyday life. Jesus—we should remember—used only the common words of the ordinary speech of his time. The scientist, the religious man, the artist, and the ordinary man or woman are dealing with basic theology if they are honestly trying to understand and to express their experience of life and of God, whatever words or means of expression they use. The three lines that we have been discussing cannot be regarded as having nothing to do with theology. If, as we probably should, we keep the name "theology" for the more technical discipline of our criticism of our experience of God, then we have to see the thinking and experience of the scientist, the religious man, the artist and ordinary people as offering the basic material with which "theology" has to deal. Without their experience theology would have nothing to discuss. For without mind, will, and imagination what is there to discuss?

Theology, in this precise sense—the sense in which we

talk about faculties and professors of theology, and theological books and theology as an examinable subject—can test our pictures of Jesus to say whether they are orthodox but cannot give us a picture of Jesus. This is why the theological names for Jesus are a puzzle and difficulty for many people. They are often used in a dead way as tests of orthodoxy and not as words to awaken our love and understanding. They have become technical terms. And technical terms in any area of knowledge are not aids to vision. They are substitutes for experience. Take a very simple example. The chemical definition of water is $H_2O$. But this is no description of water. If we had not learned the formula we would not have any idea what $H_2O$ was like. It does not tell us that water is wet, and falls from the sky as rain, and runs down the hills in streams, and forms rivers and lakes; that we can drink it and wash with it and can sail on it and drown in it—and that life depends on it. When we say that Jesus is the only Son of God we are using words in the same kind of technical way as when we define water as $H_2O$. We will understand it only if each symbol is defined and explained in other words. And we will not have any clearer a picture of Jesus in the end. And this is a very great pity for theology has taken something that was in the teaching of Jesus and reduced it to an unintelligible formula.

This perhaps need not have happened. But it did. It happened because theology from the beginning and for centuries has not been primarily concerned with Jesus as a person. It is not from Jesus that the theologians in the past began to build their systems. It has, therefore, been left to the heretics, the near-heretics, the enthusiasts, the sectarians, the artists, the poets, to recover in their own times the picture of Jesus, sometimes in exaggerated ways and often disrupting the peace of the church.

Theology has seen its task as expressing the faith of the church in ways comprehensible to the rest of men's thinking and knowledge. It has, therefore, always been conscious of contemporary thought-forms. The trouble has been that it has taken these thought-forms as primary. It has tried to fit Jesus into them. It has begun, not with Jesus as a person, but with certain absolutes. We see this both when we discuss the question of the person of Christ and when we discuss the work he achieved for men. The former discussion in the first centuries centered on the word "substance" which appears in the Nicene Creed—"of one substance with the Father." How were the two natures, human and divine, to be applied to Jesus? Of this discussion John McIntyre writes: "To put the matter quite generally, the questions at issue when Eutycheans, Nestorians, Leo, the orthodox party at Chalcedon, and Leontius of Byzantium, discuss the person of Jesus Christ, his humanity and his divinity, and how these co-exist, are not really christological questions at all, but rather logical questions about universals, how they exist, whether they can exist *in abstracto,* and how they relate to the particulars in which they are instanced . . . what may appear on the surface to be a christological controversy . . . are in fact logical or philosophical controversies about how a certain philosophical proposition is to be applied to the Christ-event." [1]

[1] "The Openness of Theology," Inaugural Lecture, New College, Edinburgh University. *New College Bulletin,* IV (Autumn 1968), p. 11.

In the same way, when the scholars of the church discussed Christ's work of salvation they did not begin with their understanding of their basic experience of what Jesus had done for men. They began with the two abstractions—sin and justice, into which what Jesus had done had to be fitted and an explanation found in the various theories of the atonement. In theories of substitution and punishment all that Jesus had done and taught was forgotten.

This old and classical theology had begun by building on these abstractions which it regarded as absolutes. And it is necessary to remember how strong has been the effect of their work and how many Christians still regard the foundation of their faith to lie in abstractions—"morality," "truth," and still "justice" and "punishment"—which they would regard as absolutes. It has to be remembered that theology is worldwide and that it existed and exists outside the Christian faith. And in the East, theology has always been concerned with the pursuit of absolutes and religion has been an escape from the personal, the incidental, and the temporal. This tradition was very strong in the world into which Christianity came. Its theology was very much influenced by philosophy and by the religions of the East. But there is an essential and unending antagonism between this kind of thinking and belief in and obedience to a person.

For the one sure thing you can say about a person is that he is neither abstract nor absolute. He is particular. He is distinct and different from everyone else. He is in one place and at one time. He is finite, dependent on the accidents of place and time, limited in his opportunities. The faith

112

of the church is based on the knowledge that Jesus was such a person and on the particular things that he did at a particular place at a particular time. The theology of the church in trying to fit him into an abstract scheme of absolutes has seemed to be insisting that Jesus was none of these things; that Jesus was not a particular man, subject to the contingencies of place and time, and victorious just because of it. Jesus has been reduced to a formula, an $x$ in the algebra of abstract bookkeeping, an unknowable symbol in a man-invented scheme of absolutes. This has caused a conflict that has always been present in the church. It is in the end the conflict between man's desire to build up a system that he can comprehend and control and the unpredictable nature of life that is found in one person and in all. This is the reason why there has always been a tension between theology and the life of the church. Theology has in the past tried to construct an abstract system. Faith has been based on men's experience of a particular person.

So we do not get much light on Jesus from formal theology and from the credal statements of the church. Jesus has been a problem to formal theology as he was to the religious teachers of his own time. An interesting example of this is to be found in a book which by its title might seem to be promising for our topic and which can certainly be regarded as a sound and scholarly exposition of the teaching of the Protestant churches in the first quarter of this century. The title on the outside—*The Person of Jesus Christ*—might lead us to think that here was a book about Jesus. The fuller title inside enlightens us—*The Doctrine of the Person of Jesus Christ*. There is very little in the book about the person we know as Jesus but a very great deal about all the philosophical systems into which theologians have tried to fit him. This is typical of the approach of theology in the past. But the book contains what are really two asides which are significant. In a footnote the author, H. R. Mackintosh, writes: "It is a striking and significant circumstance that the faith thus given to Christ is given in opposition to natural inclination. Our first impulse is not to submit but to resent keenly the condemnation passed on our sinfulness by Christ's mere presence, and to reject with a grudging envy the thought that He is higher than we." [2] We can appreciate his attitude and there is truth in it. Awe and self-condemnation are natural reactions to the sight of Jesus in his suffering. But were these the first reactions of his disciples and the common people in Galilee? Were they not first attracted by him? And was not his word to men of forgiveness rather than of condemnation? Theology has generally found it easier to accept and fit into its scheme the awful figure on the cross than the man who not only died but lived his own particular life.

The other is more important. It is really a conclusion that comes in in the by-going. Obviously Mackintosh is unsatisfied with the abstract way in which he had been forced by the theological conventions of his time to deal with his subject. He sees the need of thinking in more ethical, and therefore more personal, terms. "It is more than possible," he writes, "that by this ethicising of the Divine attributes we may relieve some of the gravest problems of the incar-

[2] H. R. Mackintosh, *The Person of Jesus Christ* (Edinburgh: T. & T. Clark, 1912), p. 352n.

nation, particularly those which are due less to ascertained facts of history than to the physical and all but mechanical thought-forms employed by the early Church." He then goes on to say: "The re-statement of Christology in fully personal and spiritual terms may be a long and exacting task; but it is unavoidable, and if carried forward on sound lines may well hope for results of a permanently valid character." [3]

The task to which he pointed as the task of the future is the urgent task of today. As he says, it is an unavoidable task. It is unavoidable if men are to see Jesus as a person and to commit themselves to him as the hope of the world. It will certainly be a long and exacting task for there is much of useless lumber to get out of our minds and above all we have to realize that we learn by action and not just by thought. And it is devoutly to be hoped that the result would be in a new certainty and clarity in our picture of Jesus. Otherwise it will have proved a pointless exercise. If successful it would be a radical revolution in the direction of theology and a new positive contribution to the thinking of the church. The task is that of Christianizing our theology.

The hopeful thing is that in the last decades there has been a revolution in theology. Theology is freeing itself from its thraldom to absolutes and abstractions. We no longer feel the attractive power of orthodoxy or of the neoorthodoxies which were more dangerous. For they were all based on the acceptance and defense of old abstract categories. We no longer dare to try to claim absoluteness for our views by calling them biblical. Theologians of today seem

[3] *Ibid.*, p. 303.

rather to want to begin with a more objective acceptance of Jesus and an understanding of man's life in the world today. In a way it is a beginning with facts rather than with theories—historical facts and psychological facts, scientific facts and social facts. And no doubt the change in theological thinking owes a great deal to the influence of modern science and the priority it gives to facts over theories.

But theological thinking can never be done in isolation. It arises out of the experience of men and women in their ordinary lives. It arises out of the life of the church if by the church we mean, as we should, the entirety of Christian men and women living their lives with all other people in the world. So the ground of theology is not what scholars do in their studies but how Christian men and women act and think together. In other words we will not be able to base our theology on Jesus until we begin deliberately to put him in the center of our living.

And yet we probably have to be a little clearer in our thinking before we feel free to act. We are hemmed in by things we take for granted even while we question them. We have to cut ourselves free by means of our questions and our convictions.

In our thinking we have to begin where Paul began, though if we are to think for ourselves today, we shall need to be prepared thereafter to follow our own way, not his. Paul wrote to the Corinthians that when he came among them he was "determined not to know any thing among you, save Jesus Christ, and him crucified" (I Cor. 2:2). He knew that this was a stumbling block to those of them who were Jews and simply madness to those of them who were Greeks. He knew that he could have persuaded them to listen to him much more easily if he had first talked to them in the language of Greek philosophy or of Jewish Law. And, of course, he did so talk later. For when Paul claimed that he would not know anything else save Jesus, he did not mean that he had no knowledge of other things or that he was not always learning more and more about the world and anxious to do so. He meant that for him now the starting point of all his knowledge of everything was Jesus. And for him that meant everything he knew about Jesus: everything that shocked them about Jesus—the fact that he had been put to death as a criminal, the fact that he had died at all; but also all that had roused him to persecute the disciples of Jesus—the simple life and the scandalous teaching of Jesus. Sometimes perhaps when we try to understand the varying ways in which Paul tried to explain to different groups of difficult people how Jesus could be related to their lives, and even more when we try to understand the schemes by which scholars have tried to bring consistency into Paul's lively thinking, we forget that for Paul everything rested on the life and teaching of Jesus and the fact that he was not dead. This was the fact into which all other facts had to fit and miraculously did fit. This was the light that illumined every other experience of life. It was in his light that he dared to look at the world, the future, and God.

In doing this Paul was asserting that the world, life and the future, and God were to be understood in personal terms and indeed in terms of one particular man—Jesus. We should never assume that this was any easier for him to do than it is for us. For Paul the blinding nature of his conversion lay not just in his vision of Jesus as eternally true but also in the recognition of what this involved. It meant for him a radical revolution in all his accepted ideas about the world and man's life and God. The disciples who had shared Jesus' life in Galilee had been led more gently to the same conviction. Paul felt that he had been "born out of due time" (I Cor. 15:8)—born into a different world, a native of Tarsus, a Roman citizen, a Pharisee of the Pharisees —and regretted that he had not shared the Galilean experience but claimed equally to share with them the vision of the risen Christ. His conversion was more a matter of intellectual and moral reorientation than was the awakening of the eleven and the women. And so it should say more to us. And indeed Paul in claiming that his vision was authentic and that he too was an apostle was not making an exclusive claim for himself to gate-crash the company of the original apostles. He was rather making a claim for all who were to follow him: that they would have to see the risen Christ in ways as different from his vision on the road to Damascus as his vision there was from that of the first disciples on the first Easter morning. For any faith that is based on persons or a person cannot be merely traditional or inherited but must always be immediate and experienced in personal life.

If we today were to try to begin to base our thinking about everything on our knowledge of Jesus, what would it mean?

It would begin with our desire and intention to see Jesus with our imagination as intimately as his contemporaries saw him with their eyes. They saw him as a particular man living his own particular life. If we regard Jesus as an abstraction, as a counter, albeit a necessary counter, in God's dealing with mankind, then it does not matter what kind of a life Jesus lived. It would be enough, as indeed some theologians of the past have declared, if the baby Jesus had breathed only one breath in the manger and had then died: the account in God's bookkeeping would have been settled. But this has nothing to do with the experience of the disciples. What they shared was the years of his ministry. What they went out to declare was "all that Jesus began both to do and to teach" (Acts 1:1). Their personal experience of him and of the life he lived is preserved for us in the four gospels. It is this personal knowledge of a person conveyed to us through the memory, knowledge, and experience of persons and therefore liable to the personal failure of memory and to ambiguities of understanding that is the basis of the church's life and faith. This is why we have always to get back to the Gospels. If we must, as Paul tells the Colossians they must, "be rooted in him and built on him," then it is of all the particularities of his life that we are to think. We have to see him, as his contemporaries saw him, as one moving about, meeting people, responding to their needs, breaking the rules, telling people that they already possessed God's kingdom, calling on them to turn their minds round and believe this, telling them stories to make them see what human life was like, telling them stories that forced them to ask questions, refusing to accept the dividing of people into the young and the old, men and women, good and bad. The first thing we always have to do, the basic thing, is to see Jesus as the man he was. We have to see the openness of his life with other people even if we are

shocked by it. Indeed perhaps we will not really notice it
unless we are shocked by it. We see a man who lived fully
the life he wanted to live, who was not deflected from it by
suffering or lack of results or thought of the future. We ask
the questions "Why": why should men suffer? Why does
evil exist? Jesus never asked these questions: not that he did
not feel the force of them, but because life was a greater thing
and contained them. Edwin Muir once wrote: "The existence of evil remains a mystery to me: I prefer that mystery
to any explanation of it that I know." [4] Jesus was more
concerned with the mystery of love, which also is to be
preferred to any explanation of it. "Love neither rules, nor
is it unmoved; also it is a little oblivious as to morals. It does
not look to the future, for it finds its own reward in the
immediate present." [5] This was what his contemporaries saw
in Jesus.

But if we are going to take Jesus seriously as the ground of
our life and of our thinking we must go farther than this.
We have to let him speak for himself. We have to take his
teaching seriously and with the emphasis that he gives it.
Of course we have our own preferences and prejudices.
Of course there are inconsistencies and even contradictions
between the four gospels. Of course we have to give our own
interpretation in the end. All this is implied in the fact that
Jesus was a person and lived with people and that we are
persons. The New Testament, the plays of Shakespeare, and
the poetry of Homer have been subjected to more continuous and closer scholarly criticism than any other books

[4] Edwin Muir, *The Story and the Fable*, p. 267.
[5] A. N. Whitehead, *Process and Reality*, pp. 520-21.

in the world. This scholarship helps greatly in our understanding of text, sources, and background. But it does not
answer the important questions: Why was the book written?
What is it saying? What does it mean? These questions can
be answered only by the reader or, better, by the actor who
acts the play on the stage, or acts the gospel in life. This
seemingly scholarly uncertainty about the text is a wonderful
excuse. But it is not the real reason why the church in its
theology has not taken Jesus' teaching as its basis, even when
the members of the church have been trying to make it the
basis of their living. The real reason is that in our thinking
we have not heeded Paul's warning: "Make sure that no
one traps you and deprives you of your freedom by some
secondhand, empty, rational philosophy based on the principles of this world instead of on Christ" (Col. 2:8 Jer.
Bible). We have tried to fit Jesus into some abstract scheme.
And the only way to fit what is personal into a scheme of
absolutes is by the elimination of all that is distinctive in
the person. And our attempt goes further. We not only
eliminate what is distinctively personal, we reduce the living
person to a dead abstraction. Absolute qualities are attributed to what is personal. Power and authority are the
qualities that we think belong to God. We are concerned
to find how Jesus may reflect them. But according to Jesus
these qualities have nothing to do with God. As A. N.
Whitehead says: "The Church gave unto God the attributes
which belonged exclusively to Caesar." [6] And we have con-
tinued by attributing them to Jesus. It is only as we accept
the reality of the life that Jesus lived and glimpse "the

[6] *Ibid.*, p. 520.

brief Galilean vision of humility" that we can accept his teaching about loving our enemies and forgiving those who do us wrong. And certainly it is only as we do this that we will understand what he is saying about God—his openness, his lack of concern about morality, his love of all men.

This means that we must give up our one great defense against taking Jesus seriously—our pity for him. Pity is a quality that belongs to a spectator. We have to be a bit detached to feel pity. Any idea of Jesus as in place of us, as a substitute, leaves us above the suffering. And the tribute we offer for our escape is pity. Jesus never asks for our pity, just as he refused the pity of the women who wept for him on the way to Calvary. He does not ask for pity because what he is doing is the life he chooses to live. He suffers because he is one of us, because he is a man and this is life and his way to live. He does not ask for our pity. He is willing to wait for our understanding and love.

And just as we sometimes arouse pity in order to get our own way, so we can use Jesus for our own ends. We use the name of "Christian" to sanctify our causes. Or we make the orthodoxy or unintelligibility of the titles we give him the excuse for our detachment from other men and our superiority to them. The blasphemy to which Christians are all too prone is an attitude of superiority to other men, to Jesus and therefore to God. The church often sees its task as being to defend God, even, in the words of Ronald Gregor Smith, "to rescue God from the consequences of his own recklessness first in creating and then in saving his world . . . as altogether too dashing, too audacious and foolhardy." [7] We try to reduce Jesus' teaching to fit in to our schemes of human wisdom. And so we defend God and pity Jesus and despise our fellowmen. And, of the three, the last would be the worst in his eyes.

It may be that if we in the church begin with our knowledge of Jesus and proceed from there to think creatively and positively about the world we now live in and the way men now live and the ways in which they must learn to live, we shall come to some new title for Jesus and some new way to describe him. The search might well take so long that the title finally adopted would then be as out-of-date as the old orthodox names now seem to us. But this is no reason for not embarking on the task. It does not matter what name we give to Jesus. At least it does not matter to him. It will not change him. It does matter to us. It can affect us. It can change us. The name we give commits us, not him. If we call him "Master" then we confess ourselves his servants. If we call him "brother" we confess ourselves to be of one family with him and with all other men. If we give him a name and do not mean it, we brand ourselves as hypocrites. But the task of trying to describe him and of seeing where he stands and how he speaks to us in our immediate situation is one that must go on. This is, at bottom, what theology is all about. The challenge to us is to begin at the beginning, with him and with the here and now, and not so far along the road that we have missed his company. We have to begin with him in all the hopes and fears, the protests and desires, the ambiguities and tensions, the violence and the achievements of human life today.

[7] Ronald Gregor Smith, *The New Man*, p. 98.

They are all about Man. The one certain thing that we know about Jesus is that he was a man. What we know about him is his willing participation in all the divisions and tensions, the fears and the hopes of the men of his day; his willingness to suffer its violence, his refusal to let protest kill love, his conviction that life was the gift of God.

The trouble is that we are terribly afraid of life. We are afraid of God's foolishness in creating man and in loving him. But we can not believe in God without believing in man. Perhaps when we talk about the death of God we really mean that we despair of the life of man. A deeper concern about man is the way to faith in God.

A personal incident is often the best way to make a point. When I went to China in 1925 and landed a stranger in Shanghai, one of the first persons I met was Dr. Cheng Ching Yi, the first great statesman of the Chinese Church and at that time the Secretary of the National Christian Council of China. I was fortunate in being introduced to the Chinese Church by him. He said many interesting things, but by far the most illuminating was his remark that he was very dissatisfied with the theology of the church in the West. In particular he felt that it had nothing to say about man. "A Chinese Creed," he added, "would have the clause: 'We believe in man.'" I remember how I, so recently a student in a theological college, received a slight shock. I said that at least we did believe in Jesus. But I felt, even then, that this did not answer his objection. Of course it should have: to believe in Jesus should obviously mean to believe in man. But he and I knew that it did not. The church in the West emphatically did not believe in man.

Indeed its belief in Jesus as the Son of God was the sign that the sons of men were beyond belief. Through the years, and especially during my years in China, I came to appreciate the profound truth of Cheng Ching Yi's remark.

But we can dare to believe in man only if we believe in Jesus. His life and teaching is the only ground for belief in man and hope for man. To believe in him is to see him as the way of life for men, the truth hidden in the mystery of all material things, and the key to life. It means to know him not just as one who once lived but who is alive in all life. It is therefore to believe in his resurrection. But it only is belief if it issues in joyful commitment to his revelation of human life. If we believe in him we give up all ideas of divisions and grades among men. We repudiate, and not with any sense of sacrifice, any desire for authority or the wish to instruct.

Men today are lost and are violent in their seeking because they know that what they really want is this kind of open acceptance among men. They are saying: "'Sir, we would see Jesus." Are we prepared to let him go free, without a name save his own name of Jesus?

We are afraid to let him go defenseless because we are afraid to be defenseless ourselves. We want to protect him by honorable titles and by outworn creeds and by incomprehensible dogma. We are still slaves to the power of abstractions. "It must be frankly confessed," wrote S. L. Frank, the Russian philosopher, "that the conception of God's absolute omnipotence, similar to the political omnipotence of an absolute monarch before whom all opposition instantly crumbles away, is a false idea and finds no confirmation either in life's experience or in actual religious feeling." [8]

We have to free ourselves from these outworn ideas of power and authority if we are to begin to see Jesus in our modern world and to be able relevantly to talk about him to other men.

We have to find him in our lives before we will find words for him.

But at least we know his name—Jesus.

[8] S. L. Frank, *God With Us*, Natalie Duddingston, trans. (Jonathan Cape, 1946), p. 197.

# Learning to Live

Today our problems are with ourselves. They are about the way we live and the kind of people we are. They are about the problem of living with the wide diversity of men and women with whom we now have to live in mutual dependence. Probably men's main problems have always been with themselves. But today we know that we cannot get outside ourselves to solve them. Our destiny is in our own hands. And we are afraid. We can fly to the moon, but we carry our own questions with us. And those questions are both much wider and more intimate than they have ever been before. We can not get away from ourselves and the problem of human life—certainly not now.

Perhaps for the first time in centuries we can understand

what it means to say that it is only in man that we can see the meaning of creation. Perhaps with our new interest in the particular rather than in the general we are beginning to appreciate, with Paul, how a particular man can be "the firstborn of every creature"—the promise of purpose and glory for all—and how he can also be the image of the invisible God"—the only way in which we can understand and believe in God (Col. 1:15). It is certainly not surprising that we should feel compelled to look around for new ways of describing Jesus which would help to indicate how central he is to our understanding of human life and of the nature of God.

Insofar as we see him alive in our world today—and this is the only way we can be said to see him and to believe in him at all—then we see him leading us into the future, into the life of the world to come. This is indeed what the experience of the Resurrection meant to the early church. It set their minds and their feet on the way into the future. For faith can never be a matter of straining our eyes to see Jesus in the distant past. For the men of the early church to know that Jesus was alive was to see all men with love and the world with hope. For us in this age, who cannot escape from the knowledge of Jesus, it may be that it is to see other men with love and the world with despair, as many poets and dramatists do, that leads us to see Jesus as the meaning of life and the hope of its glory. To see men in their suffering and hopes, their fears and their achievements today and to see Jesus living the same life in the world of his day is to realize that it is the same life. In him we understand ourselves and other men and in him we know the mystery of life, even now in its frustrations and suffering.

To see Jesus as the way into the future is to know him as our life now. For the present belongs to the future more than it belongs to the past. Our life—not just our task in life but our life—is to live his life in the world today. It can never be a life lived at secondhand by the conventions of another age. His life is always a new life, and men have never lived in our present world before.

For this Jesus called men and continues to call men. But he has never sent them out into the world as solitary individuals. His first disciples had to learn to live with him and with each other before he sent them out to live as persons in the world. And since then the church is—or should be— the place where we learn to live as persons in the world of our day.

So before we think of Jesus in our world and our place with him there, we think of the church and Jesus' place in it. It is right to think of this first because this is where most of us begin. Our knowledge of Jesus has come to us through the church, our Christian life is due to the church. And for those who are outside the church it is to the church that they look for their picture of Jesus. Sometimes they look in expectation, for they hope to see him more clearly. Often they are depressed and offended by what they see. But still it is to the church that they look. So it is right to begin with the church, with the question what a new vision of Jesus would mean for the church and how it can be a place where we learn to live as persons in the world today. It is right to take this first to remind us that what comes after is the final test.

But what is the church? Men have given many definitions of the church. They have used many pictures and metaphors to describe it. But whatever definition we favor, two things are unquestionably certain about the church and basic to every definition of it. One is that the church is made up of persons. The other is that it is founded on one person— Jesus. The church is thus personal through and through, human in its composition, personal in its origin and purpose. This doubly personal character of the church makes it unique among all the institutions of human society.

It is the fact that the church is made up of people that differentiates Christianity from the great religions of the East. There is common matter to compare in sacred books, theology, priesthood, and architecture. But there is nothing in these religions with which we can compare the church. Jesus did not write a book or construct a theology or build a building or institute a priesthood. But he did call people. People are primary because Jesus acted in history to lead men into their history.

It shares this serious view of the material world and belief in God's purpose in history with Judaism and Islam, for all three spring from the root of Old Testament acceptance of the material world and of history. And so it has often been in conflict with them. And it can be, and often is, classified with the secular organizations of men. A nation, a factory, an army, a school, a hospital are all likewise made up of people. It is possible, and sometimes quite valuable, to compare the church with them in the way of its working.

But the second personal characteristic of the church differentiates it from all these other organizations. These are all founded and continue to exist for a particular purpose, which is obvious and can be stated. They need their members to serve these purposes. An army exists to wage war. If war were abolished, there would be no point in an army. A political party exists to attain and then to exercise power. A factory exists to produce a certain product. If there is no longer a demand for it, its workers become redundant. The church is not founded on a cause or a policy or the manufacture of a product. Often it is judged because it is seen to be serving or not to be serving some such purpose. Sometimes it has indeed seen its function to be doing such things. It has tried to be the nation. It has acted as a political party. It has seen itself as an agent of welfare and has run schools and hospitals and taken on the care of those in need. And, of course, it is right that Christians should be engaged in such activities. Sometimes it is the duty of the church to initiate them because there is no one else ready to do them. But these are not the purposes for which the church exists. "Who built the Church at Dunscore? " Thomas Carlyle asked. And he answered his own question, "Jesus Christ built the Church at Dunscore." Of course, someone founded the Church at Dunscore centuries ago. And someone built the first church building. And someone built the present one. And people in the past have been the church there and other people are the church there now. There would have been no church if it had not been for all these innumerable men and women and children. But, far more fundamentally, there would have been no idea of a church, no desire to form a church, no tradition to continue it, no church at all, if it had not been for Jesus. The abiding, unchangeable purpose of the church is summed up in him. The church exists solely because Jesus lived and taught and died and lives, and because he brought men and women into his life and still does so. It would be wrong to say that the church's purpose is to live Christ's life in the world as the purpose of a shipbuilding yard is to build ships. The living of the life of Jesus is not the end product which sometimes may be accomplished. It is its life now as much as it ever was or ever will be. In the living of his life we have to get back to Jesus and the life he lived on earth. But the church must live fully in the setting of today because its members are living today in this world. To live according to the pattern of a former day is ritualism not life. Jesus is as much the man for our day as he was for Paul's, because he lived man's life and lived it well. Paul wrote that his life has to be made manifest in our mortal flesh (II Cor. 4:11). He meant that it has to be lived in us as persons, at this present time, in the secular setting of our lives. And that was as hard a task then as it is now.

This is the life we are called to live. We cannot live it without thought and will. This involves us in seeing Jesus and in seeing the world in which we live and in seeing them meeting in us as persons. This will lead us out into all kinds of activities and associations. These are necessary but secondary because always changing. Among these, high place must be given to the task of helping other people see Jesus as he is in the world today. But whether we do this depends on whether the church is living the life of Jesus and not just an efficient church-centered life, for only so will its members be seeing Jesus themselves.

The church has at times got so engrossed in its own institutional activities or its theology that it has been unaware that its life lies elsewhere—with Jesus in the world. These are often the times to which Christians in time of stress and confusion look back with envy. They see them as periods of peace, stability, and power for the church, when the mass of the people claimed church membership and the church dominated society and told men what to do and "nothing told me that Christ was born in the flesh and had lived on earth." The pity is that we regard these as the great days of the church. The miracle is—and we can attribute it only to the grace of God—that the face of Jesus has never been totally obscured from men, that somehow he has always revealed his presence in strange places. And certain it is that it has been in times of crisis, when society is shaken and new ways open to men, when men are in doubt and confusion and despair, that men have seen Jesus for themselves and found his way a challenge, a rebuke, and a comfort.

Today is certainly such a time. And men outside the church are discovering Jesus for themselves. But what is the church doing? Are we as Christians living the life of Jesus in some new, fresh, joyful, confident way? Do men see Jesus more clearly and more adequately because of our life in the church today?

If we cannot give an honest, affirmative answer to this question, then we must ask ourselves what is wrong. Is it the vision that is lacking? Or the intention? Or are we just confused?

Perhaps it would help if we began by asking what are the

things in the church that obscure Jesus from ourselves and therefore from other men.

There are some features in the church's life today which we take for granted and even justify but which certainly obscure and distort the picture of Jesus that we reflect to men.

First of all there is our authoritarianism. It is authoritarianism rather than authority—the conviction that we have a right to be heard rather than the authority of conviction in what we say. The ordinary man is not so inconsistent as he sounds when at one and the same time he wants the church to say something and resents what the church seems to be saying. For what the church seems to be doing is telling people what they ought not to be doing and to be using its power to prevent them doing what they want. This is authoritarianism—the assumed right to instruct, to impose patterns of behavior and of thought on other people. It is, in the end, the claim to the right to persecute. It has nothing to do with the authority that men recognized in Jesus. His was the authority that has nothing to do with authoritarianism. He dispensed with all the sanctions of power. He would do nothing to enforce belief. And because his authority was the unchanging truth of love, he was prepared to die. And men recognize this authority, but of their own free will.

The church in all its denominations is beginning today to abandon some of its authoritarian attitudes. This is partly because it realizes that it lives in a changed world. Men have learned to be suspicious of authoritarian statements, because they live in an age of advertisement and have grown to take dogmatic statements with a pinch of salt, and also because they are better educated and have learned to ask questions. The church is beginning to realize that it cannot merely tell people what to believe and what to do. But this retreat from authoritarianism is due also to the fact that the church is being forced by events to find where its basic faith lies. It is, in some quarters, becoming uncomfortably aware that it has not been taking Jesus very seriously.

But still the image of authoritarianism remains, in the minds of many outside the church and in the opinions and actions of many of its members. And it obscures men's view of Jesus.

Secondly, there is the church's aloofness. It wants to be seen as different from other people. Of course the demands that Jesus makes are stiff, and those who follow them are different from many other people. But there was nothing aloof about Jesus in his life on earth. The only people he quarreled with were the religious leaders of his day. Otherwise there was no barrier between him and other people. They were at home with him. He shared their life fully. This was what offended the leaders. And this is the one characteristic of Jesus that has constantly been expressed in all the varied pictures that men have made of him down the ages. But the church seems still to be cautioning its members not to get mixed up with other people, to remain apart, aloof, superior. Sometimes this is called "making a witness."

We might call the next obscuring quality respectability; conformity with traditional conventions and attitudes. But some kind of conformity with the society in which we live is inevitable. And lack of conformity may also be a sign of detachment and aloofness from other people. Respectability in its modern use is a very relative term. It can be good, and it can be bad. The quality in the church that obscures Jesus is rather the attitude that feels that it deserves respect —the conviction that the church should be treated with deference, that its views should be accepted without it having to say very much, that it has a right to the comfortable and honorable seats. And sometimes the church seems to regard these signs of respect as the symbols of its authority, to be defended at all costs. In this the church seems to have traveled very far from Jesus.

Perhaps the greatest contrast that men see between Jesus and the church is in the matter of money. The church at all times of its history, except in the first century of its life anywhere, has always been good at gathering money. In many countries the church holds vast property in land and investments. And the one thing that most people know about the church is that it is always asking for money. Men are not surprised that the church should need money for they need it themselves. They are not surprised that in our more affluent societies the church should need more money than ever before. This is not what puzzles men. They do not expect the church to advocate poverty. They know that Jesus fed people and told his followers to share with others and spoke of the day when all these things would be added unto them. They are puzzled because they do not see any of this reflected in the church's attitude to money.

Does the accumulation of wealth in the church and its investment in capitalistic enterprises not tie the church to the present economic structure of the West? Does this and its hoarding of its resources for its economic security in the future and its primary concern for the upkeep of its buildings and institutions not prevent any real sharing with others, especially with those with no security at all? Why does the church always seem to put its own needs first?

And then there is the wistful wonder whether the church with Jesus' teaching and its own great resources might not make in itself some kind of economic experiment that might show men how they could live together in a world of peace and plenty.

But, as it is, the church's use of its own money and especially its very efficiency drops a steel grill to shut off the picture of Jesus.

Does this authoritarian, aloof, respectable, prosperous body give to men the reflection of the man to whom it owes its existence? The fact that it is not corrupt and does good work almost makes it more difficult for men to see that it has anything to do with one who offended the respectable and was put to death as a political agitator.

The church or the Christian cannot with any confidence decide how he is going to draw the picture of Jesus for others to see. What the church or the Christian is committed to is the intention of learning to live the life of Jesus now. Unless the church is doing this it is no true church. Unless a Christian is doing this he is no Christian at all. It is to this that mind, will, and imagination have to be given. The reality of any picture of Jesus that he conveys to men depends on his sincerity in this. When he comes to speak about Jesus he will however have to be careful not to use words that are meaningful and even dear to himself but are quite misleading to other people.

What, then, should the church be doing? We use the word "church" with all kinds of meanings—a building, a congregation, a denomination, the clergy, the hierarchy, the whole body of Christians throughout the world. The word "church" is only used twice in the Gospels, both times in Matthew's Gospel, and in each case the exact meaning is not very certain. Jesus did not talk about the church, but he did talk about how his followers were to live and this is surely the same thing.

Some of the things that he says about the life of his followers seem contradictory. He offers an open invitation to all and is ready to welcome them without precedence or priority of race, creed, or morality. At the same time, he says that the gate is very narrow and that many will be turned back. In the thirteenth chapter of Luke's Gospel the two ideas are set side by side. He says:

Strive to enter in at the strait gate: for many, I say unto you, will seek to enter in, and shall not be able.

When once the master of the house is risen up, and hath shut to the door, and ye begin to stand without, and to knock at the door, saying, Lord, Lord, open unto us; and he shall answer and say unto you, I know you not whence ye are; Then shall ye begin to say, We have eaten and drunk in thy presence, and thou hast taught in our streets.

But he shall say, I tell you, I know you not whence ye are; depart from me, all ye workers of iniquity. (Luke 13:24-27)

138

## Learning to Live

And Jesus goes on immediately to say:

> And they shall come from east, and from the west, and from the north, and from the south, and shall sit down in the kingdom of God.
> And, behold, there are last which shall be first, and there are first which shall be last. (Luke 13: 29-30)

Which description is of the church? Is the church the one great open society, or is it a closed community of dedicated people? And how do we reconcile the two views? In general we hold the two together by assuming that we have received the invitation and can count on reserved seats but that a stringent demand must be made on those who are outside. So we talk a lot about stepping up the conditions for entrance but not so much about the demands on those who are inside. The way Jesus held them together was the exact opposite. The invitation is to all men without distinction; the demand and the judgment are on those who deliberately enter into the new life. We cannot say which group Jesus saw as the church. All we can say is that he was concerned with both. We can also admit that it is quite unfair. Why should those who are willing to go farther receive the greater condemnation? The paradox which seems so unfair is the paradox inherent in all life. The seed that is buried grows and bears fruit. It is also the paradox of the gospel—he who went farthest is crucified.

If we take the church to be made up of those for whom the life of Jesus is life, then the church in its life must express the two ideas that Jesus held together. It must be the means of expressing Jesus' open invitation to all men, without distinction of race, creed, or morality. This invitation is not into the church but into life—the life of Jesus in the world. This life can be defined as liberty, freedom from all that prevents men's progress into a world where all men are equal and at peace. At the same time the church must be prepared to serve this purpose. This would mean that the church should be prepared to be misunderstood and opposed and condemned. It would mean loving and suffering as Jesus loved and suffered. It could only be done if the church was glad to live this kind of life. It would mean departing from any comfortable idea that Jesus died on the cross that we might escape suffering.

The church is committed to openness and love because it is founded on Jesus. These are the marks of the church just as much as "the true Preaching of the Word" and "the right administration of the Sacraments" and "Ecclesiastical discipline uprightly ministered" as the reforming authors of the Scots Confession of 1560 noted them. Indeed a willingness to accept all men and a love for them extending even to the loving of our enemies would seem to be more distinctively the notes of Jesus and of his church than concern about the rigid ordering of the institution of the church. This openness and the intention to love we should expect to see in all the visible manifestations of the church. Openness is so obvious a thing that it might even be written into the constitution of every church organization. Love is a more difficult thing to enforce by legislation. Jesus did indeed give his disciples a new command to love each other, but he gave this command after he had given a lot of other commands—to follow him, to go out, to forgive each other.

They had had to go through quite a training before he could tell them to love each other. For it is no use giving an order until it can be obeyed. The mark of the church can never be perfect obedience. But it is more than the motive. Good motives have been the excuse for many bad deeds. The mark of the church is the intention to act in love; the determination in every situation to act the love of Jesus, no matter how incomplete the act may be.

How, then, do this openness and this intention to love work out in the things that the church does and is seen to do in its worship and in its activities?

Worship is probably the part of the church's life that has most formative influence on its members and gives those outside their clearest impression of what the church is all about. So it is worth asking whether the first impact that worship makes on people is that it shows forth Jesus and leads men into his way of life. Does it proclaim Jesus, and does it relate him to the life of men in the world today?

We cannot generalize about the hundreds of thousands of places of worship in the world today. What we have to ask ourselves is whether the door is as open as Jesus' welcome was to men and women in Palestine. And whether the building impresses by its recall to the vision of Galilean humility or by its witness to the power and wealth of the congregation in previous decades? We might ask what the decoration speaks of and what the memorials commemorate, and whether silence and the exclusion of any who might make a noise is the way we remember him to whom the sick and the children came in the Temple after he had cleansed it. Is the worship of the church primarily for other people, for children and the delinquent, the seekers and the disgruntled, and for those who know that they are committed to him, a training place in their acceptance of all other men?

Worship which is an esoteric ritual for a few can never be in the name of Jesus. This does not mean that worship will ever be widely popular or that it is not worship when only two or three are gathered together. But it does mean that what we are doing in any act of worship is open to all and is for those outside rather than for the initiates, just because it is in the name of Jesus.

Color, music, art have their place in worship—but not to accentuate authority or to dress up mystery, but rather as a means by which a wide variety of people can bring their specific gifts as an offering. And it does not matter whether they are members of the church or not. But the important thing about worship is not what is brought into it but what goes out. There is, perhaps, a place in the church for the discussion of the domestic affairs of the church, but it should not be in the worship of the church. The worship of the church has to do with the world outside, the ordinary world of ordinary men, just as Jesus was concerned about that world in his day. And the message of the church is still the message of his teaching, as compelling and as strange now as it was then. The proclamation of Jesus must be as uncomfortable, and as compelling, to those inside the church as to those outside.

We need to humanize the worship of the church. We shall do that only by concentrating on Jesus. Worship becomes quite inhuman when it has to do with us, the members of the church; when it expresses our prejudices, our principles, our morals; when it is concerned to keep other people out; when its symbols are the membership roll and the closed door. In the worship of the church we have always to be on our guard against the idolatry of self-worship. Jesus alone can save us from that.

But our worship is conditioned by the life of the church. So what about the activities of the church, all the innumerable meetings, societies, groups in which the church carries on its life, all the things that take place in church halls and offices? These do not often give an impression of openness or of the intention of love for other people except at a very remote range. This is in a way inevitable and even right if we recognize the purpose of these activities. The Christian life is lived in the secular world—in the jobs people do, in their homes, in life with their neighbors, in school and club, in political activities, in sport and entertainment. The interior life of the church has only one purpose: to educate its members for their Christian life in that world. The purpose of the church's activities is not to provide a substitute life over against the real life of the world. More emphatically it is not to provide a "Christian" life over against the secular life of the world. We are not in the church to learn to live in the church. We are in the church to learn to live in the world, our contemporary world. In our ordinary education and in any kind of occupational training we are isolated with our age group; we play at experiments; we do odd things. We put up with this because we know that later we will get responsibility and have to act on our own. The life of the church may sometimes seem isolated, though rarely experimental. This is all right so long as all its activities are seen as helping people to educate themselves to live in the world.

St. Benedict spoke of his monastery as a "School in the Lord's Service." How would we see the church as a school in the service of Jesus in our very different world of today?

The first thing that we have to do is to recognize the world of today. No one would claim that it is an easy world or a stable world or a world without challenge and opportunity or other than a truly terrifying world. What we cannot say is that it is an impersonal world, though this is a phrase that church people often use. Those who complain about the world being impersonal live privileged lives in the affluent sections of the developed countries. They live at a time and in places where there is probably more opportunity for the individual and greater challenge in relationships with other persons than there has ever been before. The complaint that the world is now impersonal is at bottom the timid complaint that the world is changing and is becoming too demanding in new personal relationships.

Complaint is one thing. Protest is another. Complaint comes from fear. Protest arises from the faith and hope that life can be personal in ways yet unrealized: that life in our developed communities could be much more personal and young people, in particular, could have a greater share in participation and responsibility, and that we cannot rest till in the poorer countries there is chance for a more personal life for all.

Jesus lived what we believe was the perfectly personal life. He lived it in what we today would call very underprivileged conditions though with advantages denied to millions in South America and India today. What he did as one without privilege in an oppressed country was to show in his life that despite all he and other men suffered, the world was personal and to enable men to live in it creatively, with faith and hope and love.

And what he did with his first disciples has relevance for the life of the church today. He taught them to see the world, other people, and themselves with his eyes. He taught them to accept each other and to share life not only with him but with each other, and this they found the hardest part of his teaching. He taught them not to be concerned about their individual position, to accept change, to give up their desire to call anything their own, to go out into the world knowing that it was God's.

It took the disciples quite a long time to learn his lesson. We do not really begin any farther along the road. We need not expect that we'll train ourselves for our life in the world very quickly. But what we have to do is to see that any activity in the church is geared to this job of preparing men and women to live in tomorrow's world not yesterday's.

And the world is always the world of other people. And probably our training for Jesus' service in God's world of other people has to be done not only with other people in mind but with them. It is very pleasant to be in a cozy, little company of like-minded people but we rarely learn anything there. And in any case, it is not a description of the church.

We in the church have to be free in our relations with other people—free from set social patterns, free to understand

and to learn. We have to learn to share life with other people—to share not their ultimate hopes but their daily life.

It may well be that the church will have to begin with kindergarten lessons with its own people. This is all right and the proper place to begin so long as we realize that it is the beginning of an education that will lead us out into the adult world. We have a lot to learn about the living of the life of Jesus in the world. For one thing we have come to regard sharing as impersonal. Perhaps we will have to begin by confessing that we would have found much of Jesus' teaching impersonal. The self-denial he demanded of his followers was really the discovery of a new dimension in the meaning of the word "personal." The work of the church today may be seen as that of helping men and women to live as persons with other persons in our new interpersonal world.

In his "Christmas Oratorio" W. H. Auden makes the three wise men explain why they followed the star that led them to Bethlehem. The first says:

> To discover how to be truthful now
> Is the reason I follow this star.

The second says:

> To discover how to be living now
> Is the reason I follow this star.

The third says:

> To discover how to be loving now
> Is the reason I follow this star.

Learning to Live

And then, to sum up, they all say together:

> To discover how to be human now
> Is the reason we follow this star.[1]

To learn how to be human now is our task in the world to-day. The church should be the place of our initial training.

[1] From *Collected Poetry of W. H. Auden,* by permission of Random House and Faber & Faber.

# To Be Human Now

The names that men have given to Jesus in the past have been enlightening and we will continue to use them in the church so long as we sing their hymns and rejoice to be their heirs. But as we examine them today, they are far from satisfying our hearts or our minds. They do not measure up to what we know of Jesus and understand of his work. And they are not fully or directly relevant to our situation. They demand explanation—historical, sociological, theological. And what has to be explained cannot be said to be immediately relevant. Certainly they cannot be our answer to Jesus' question: 'Whom do you say that I am? "

Our difficulty is not that we see Jesus less clearly than men have seen him in the past. We of this century probably know more about Jesus than did the men of any other century since the first. We certainly know much more about the world he lived in and the life he lived and the words he spoke than did the men of the Middle Ages or of the Reformation. But to know about a man is not necessarily to know him. So our difficulty is not that we do not know enough about Jesus to see clearly. Neither is it that what we know about him is confusing. The remarkable thing is that Jesus seems to make the same impact on those in any age who try to look at him. The answer we must give to the first question that Jesus asked: "Whom do people say that I am?" is not very different from the answer the original disciples had to give. Men today see him as a martyr, as a symbol of suffering humanity, as a man who loved, as the only sign of hope for the world. Our difficulty in giving a name to Jesus is their difficulty. It is not that we do not know enough about Jesus or know too much about him. Our difficulty is that we do not know how to define "Man."

Today we know far more about Man than in any previous age. We know about his remote history and development. We study, as never before, his social relationships in tribe, family, nation. We study the development of his control over his environment and his social and political growth. We know a lot about how his mind and his emotions work. But we are only the more uncertain of how to define Man. To most of us the person one is never seems to fit in to these studies of Man. They are about other people, people in the abstract. They do not describe me or the people I know. Now that we know so much more about ourselves we are far from coming any nearer to a definitive answer to the question: What is man? The mystery of man has only become greater. Through our expanding exploration of the universe, we know, in a new and intense way, both the smallness of man and the wonder that he alone is the explorer. And the mystery is not only of his place in his environment, it is about himself, about what he is in himself. Behind all the political collisions of men today, behind their protest against so much of the life they live, behind their demands for a new way of life that is free and creative, there lies the conviction that man is other than his life allows. The more man knows about himself the more he searches for the meaning of his life. And the quest holds no hope of ending. As Karl Jaspers writes: "The very fact that we do not know what man really is, is an essential part of our humanity." [1] Whenever man has thought at all he has been aware of this insoluble mystery. In the Old Testament the book of Job gives the most pessimistic expression of it:

Let the day perish wherein I was born, and the night in which
    it was said, There is a man child conceived.
Let that day be darkness; let not God regard it from above. . . .
Let darkness and the shadow of death stain it. (Job 3:3-5)

In the Psalms the question is put more hopefully, but it is still a question:

What is man, that thou art mindful of him? and the son of man
    that thou visitest him?
For thou hast made him a little lower than the angels, and has
    crowned him with glory and honour.

[1] Karl Jaspers, *The Origin and Goal of History*, Michael Bullock, trans. (Yale University Press, 1968), p. 35.

## To Be Human Now

Thou madest him to have dominion over the works of thy hands;
thou hast put all things under his feet. (Psalm 8:4-6)

And Shakespeare, combining the two attitudes, makes
Hamlet muse:

"What a piece of work is a man! How noble in reason! How
infinite in faculty! In form and moving how express and ad-
mirable! In action how like an angel! In apprehension how like
a god! The beauty of the world! The paragon of animals! And
yet, to me, what is this quintessence of dust? "

This is the same question that men ask today, and perhaps
with an even greater urgency. It is the theme of the poets,
the dramatists, the novelists, the film directors. It lies behind
the violent actions of men. And those who ask the question
do not expect a verbal answer. They know that mystery is
part of our humanity. They are not looking for an answer
that will sweep away any of the mystery. For anything that
lessens the mystery reduces our stature. What they are trying
to do is to enter more deeply into the mystery.

If we could find a definitive description of Man we
would have no difficulty in giving a definite title to Jesus.
But we cannot and probably never will. Karl Barth said,
"Man is the creature made visible in the mirror of Jesus
Christ." [2] This is a profound remark, but it sets the mystery
even deeper and makes the attempt to find a title for Jesus
all the more difficult. Jesus as the mirror in which we see
Man! Men have seen their cruelty reflected in the suffering
of Jesus. They have seen their unworthiness reflected in his

[2] Alexander Miller, *The Man in the Mirror* (New York: Doubleday), p. 5.

*151*

love. It is a very different thing to say that we see ourselves reflected in his love and in his suffering. In him we learn about ourselves, even if only "as in a glass darkly." In him we see more fully the mystery of our humanity.

When we try to escape from the mystery and try to define "Man," we reduce him to an object. It is right that we should study our history as fully as possible, that we should try to understand our ways of thinking and our ways of living together. But in so doing we do not get any nearer to knowing what we are. "Sociology, psychology and anthropology," writes Karl Jaspers, "teach that man is to be regarded as an object concerning which something can be learned that will make it possible to modify this object by deliberate organization. In this way one comes to know something about man, without coming to know man himself; yet man, as a possibility of a creature endowed with spontaneity, rises in revolt against being regarded as a mere result." [3] It is only fair to these scientific disciplines to add that theology has often seemed also to regard man as an object: the object of God's creation, of his salvation, of his judgment. Indeed this is inevitable, for we can theorize only about objects. We know that we can never see ourselves as objects. We can't help rebelling against all who attempt so to treat us. Indeed the teaching of Jesus can well be interpreted as such a rebellion. This spontaneity, this innate conviction of being a subject and not an object is part of the mystery of human life. It's expressed in our talking about the spirit of man or the spirit of God. It's implied in the state-

[3] Karl Jaspers, *Man in the Modern Age* (New York: Doubleday, 1951), p. 174.

ment in Genesis that man is made in the image of God. We know that we cannot solve the mystery of human life by a definition that can only be made of an object. We can only enter more deeply into the mystery by accepting life and living it.

In the same way the attempt to give Jesus a definitive title can be carried out only by treating him as an object. Of course we must go on talking about him and trying to describe how we see him and how we understand his relationship to us and his demands on us. And we have got to use words and names to do so. But we can only safely do so when we admit the inadequacy of all our words and refuse any search for a final form of words.

The titles of authority that men in the past have given to Jesus offend us today largely because they treat us as objects. They express the idea of Jesus having done something for us. Now no one who believes in Jesus would deny that what he has done for him is beyond understanding and beyond words. But it is something into which a man enters freely. Titles like "King," "Priest," "Savior" breathe today an air of totalitarian power. We resent being treated as material in the hands of power.

Then there are the titles that seem to regard Jesus as an object for us. These are the titles before which we can put the adjective "my" such as "my Shepherd," "my Friend," "my Savior." These tend to imply that Jesus is something we possess—that he can be of use to us. And this palpably is an inadequate description.

Then there are the titles we played with because they seemed to express the relationship he wanted men to have with him: "servant," "friend," "brother." They were attractive because they expressed his unity with us. There are also the names he did not use but which would have a significant meaning for us today, such as "worker" or even "representative," as suggested by Dorothee Sölle. These are all illuminating but not very satisfactory as they express only partial relationships even though they express his essential unity with us. They also leave out his wider purposes.

So perhaps the quest of a new definitive name is hopeless. We should be glad to be free of it. This does not mean that we do not give him a name or cannot say what he is.

The only name we can use with confidence is his own name, the name to which he answered as a child and as a man, the name under which he was crucified—Jesus. And the only description we can give to him without question is that of a man.

The name "Jesus" ties us to a particular man living a particular life in a particular place. It ties us to the belief that in Jesus and in his total life we enter fully into the mystery of God and of man. This is the belief on which the Christian faith is built and from which we depart at our peril.

The name "Jesus" recalls us to the life he lived and where he lived it. His was a life of ordinary human circumstance—of home and work, of friends and enemies, of hunger, thirst, and death. He lived his life in the world, not in the church. He lived his life in the world with full acceptance, without regret or pining for another time or place or life. It calls us always back into the world, the ordinary world of other men and of God.

It reminds us also that his teaching was for the world, not just for the church. He was not saying how Christians should live, but how men should live. In his parables he showed men what life—their life in the world—was like. For all their strangeness, the stories he told were about the life they knew. He said that God's kingdom was like the life they lived, in its mystery and its presence. He taught men how they should live with others if they were to enter fully into God's kingdom in this world. His teaching was not a code of conduct for a religious society but the way for the world, based on the mystery of life.

The name of Jesus also recalls to us what he did for men: how his first disciples through their life with him and their conviction that he was still with them in the world, were able in his name to go out into the world: not to win men into a little society, but to declare that Jesus was alive and had opened the way of life to all men.

And the only certain description we can give of Jesus is that he was a man. The inevitable retort will be, "But surely not only a man?" Can we say of anyone that he is "only a man"? We do not know what Man is. We find man more and more difficult to define. We know indeed that any definition takes something from the essential mystery of human life. For every definition is static and assumes a static view of human life. And man is not static, whether we think of a person or of humanity. As persons we know that we are always in the process of learning, changing, adapting ourselves to other persons, to new situations, to our hopes, or to our laziness. We know that there is always the possibility of our becoming new, free persons. This is

the mystery of life. We know that it is true of all men and
of mankind. The only way we can know what life is and
what Man is, is by living with other people. It is only in
our life, through the life of a man living this life of ours
that we can learn what a man is and what life is. It is the only
way we can learn, for it is the only way in which we are ourselves involved. And this is what the Christian faith is all
about. This was what the early church fought to maintain
—that Jesus was a man, not someone different from all other
men, a freak. He reveals to us what man is—not in a definition, not in a dogma, not in a principle, but in a life
lived with other men. In the metaphor of Karl Barth, he
holds the mirror up to man. So that Philip Berrigan, the
American poet and Jesuit, can say: "Becoming a man is becoming what Christ was."

Here is illustrated the radical change that has taken place,
or rather is taking place, in our thinking. From the second
century to last century Christian thinkers have not begun
with man. They have begun from the other end. They have
begun with God, with God's mighty works, with Jesus as
the Son of God who became man but who above all is the
revelation of God to us. We in this century with our new
self-consciousness begin with man, with Jesus as the one
who reveals man to us and who through this revelation of
man brings us to see God. We are, strangely, much more
in the position of his contemporaries and his first disciples
who knew him first as a man and found him leading them into a new understanding of human life and to a revolutionary
view of God as their Father.

This is a very profound change. It is a radical change in

that it gets back to the root of the gospel. The accepted teaching of the church down the centuries has begun with God and with Jesus as his revelation and with the church as his body, and it never really got down to saying much about Man except that he was a miserable sinner. We have to begin with Jesus, with his revelation in life of what a man is, with the meaning of this for the world now and with the faith in God to which he leads us. If the failure of the older line was that it dealt inadequately with Man, the danger of our modern and quite inevitable approach is that we may never get to God. But for us at this time it is the best way to proceed, as well as the original.

It is our privilege to call him Jesus because he is one of us and we are able to be one with him. We know him as a man. This does not mean that he was not a teacher and a healer, a prophet and a martyr. But when we talk of him in these ways we are apt to think of him for the things he did for us and for the use we can make of him. When we think of him as a man we think of all that he was in himself. As a man we see him as the man that we should all be becoming. It is not as a teacher or a prophet or a martyr that he is the new man, but just as a man. It is as a man that we see him as the key to the pattern of man's becoming and can talk of him in terms of the purpose of man's life and its hope. It is as a man and only as a man that we can speak of him in terms of God.

But the name we give him does not affect him. It comes back on us. It reveals what we want him to be for us, and it commits us, not him. When men gave him titles of authority like "King" and "Lord" and "Conqueror," they committed themselves to unquestioning obedience. They also liked the idea that they could lord it over other men. An authoritarian theology is reflected in a hierarchical structure in the church. Men later used more personal names like "Jesus," "my Shepherd," "Husband," "Friend" because they wanted to believe in him with personal devotion. They also wanted to enjoy a quiet life.

When we today echo the salutation of Pilate "Behold the Man," we do so because we know that what baffles us is the mystery of human life and what challenges us with terrifying urgency is how we are to live together as men in the world today. We know that unless we can see meaning in human life and hope in man, it is irrelevant to talk about God. Our seeking is larger than the old desire for authority and the later quest for personal devotion. Indeed our seeking excludes these. We cannot find the meaning of our life and hope for the future without the abandonment of any domination of authority. And an intense interest in personal devotion may be a barrier to the finding of interpersonal ways of living with other men. Our seeking is also far more demanding.

To call Jesus "Man" commits us to human life. In the words of W. H. Auden we have "to discover how to be human now." This is indeed something that we have to discover. We are all human beings but we are not living human life as we wish it could be lived, far less as Jesus has revealed life to us. We like to list all the things that prevent life from being really human. We talk about the impersonality of industry, the interference of governments, and the lack of personal privacy. No one will deny there are dangers here.

But our difficulty in being human now does not lie here. It does not lie in anything that other people can do to us. Indeed the things we make our excuse are all things for which we are in our own way responsible, the fruits of which we could not easily do without. Our difficulty lies in our reluctance to live a personal life with other persons in the world. We have to go back to Jesus. He lived a fully personal life in conditions which would make us squirm. He did not complain of the difficulties that prevented his doing what he wanted, though these difficulties included death. But he was concerned all the time to destroy the things that prevented other people from living a personal life.

The first demand on us is that we follow Jesus into the world, the world in which he lived, the world of other people. It is there that life is lived. It is there alone that we can be human—or Christian, which is the same thing. We must not wait till it is safe to be human. In other words we do not wait until other people decide to be human first. Rather we accept suffering as part of the mystery of being human. Jesus did not live and die that we might be saved from suffering, however we define that suffering—as punishment for our sins or hell or what have you. He lived and died and lives now that we might live his human life. And there is no life without striving and suffering. To be human now is not to escape into an easy life. It is to live his life in the world now. And his life can never be lived in any little self-contained community we can create whether it be our home or our church or any fellowship of like-minded people. It is only in the world with all other men that we can be human now. It is only there that we can be Christian now. For it is only there that we shall see the meaning and the hope that is in Jesus.

And, of course, there will be striving and there will be suffering: suffering for us and striving on behalf of others.

Our calling of Jesus by his name and our recognition of him as Man mean that we see him in the same relation to all other people as he is to us. Bonhoeffer saw Jesus as the man "for me." He also saw him as the man "for others." Usually we try to differentiate between the two. When we think of Jesus "for me" we think of our awareness of what he has done for us. When we think of Jesus "for others" we mean that he could be the same for them. He is for others in hope. And, of course, there is a clear difference in the attitude to Jesus of those who know what he has done for them and the attitude of those who may not even know his name. But it is of our attitude and the attitude of other people that we are thinking. We are thinking about ourselves and in particular we want to be sure of what makes us different. And such a way of thinking does not mean anything if we are talking about Jesus. If we can talk about his attitude then all we can say with certainty is that his attitude to us is the same as his attitude to other men. His meaning, his teaching, his hope, his love: all that is summed up for us in Jesus the Man was the same for all. When Paul said that in him was "neither Jew nor Greek, male nor female, bond nor free" he did not mean that people were excluded from his purpose because of their jobs or their sex or their nationality. He meant that Jesus was for

160

all, irrespective of all the divisions that we build up to prevent us from being fully human.

And we cannot live this human life with other persons unless we give up our desire to dominate them. We have to accept their liberty rather than defend our own. We can be human only if we are free to exist in a continual process of becoming free. We know this in ourselves. We have to accept it for other people, in their personal and in their social lives. It is this liberty of men and women to become persons that makes it impossible for us to try to take the mystery out of life or to find a definitive statement of what man is or to give a final, static title to Jesus. This is why "Man" is the only revealing title to give him. It sets us on the way to become human ourselves. It commits us to Jesus' life of faith, hope, and love with other people.

But, of course, we cannot believe in Jesus and think that an attitude is enough, even if it is a loving attitude to all other men. We cannot attend to Jesus without realizing that what matters is what we do and not what we say. What matters to him is what we do in the world, not what we say in the church. We have only to remember the parable of the Sheep and the Goats, the last parable that Jesus spoke according to Matthew's Gospel. What matters is not whether something is done in his name but that something is done—to feed the hungry and clothe the naked and free the prisoner. This means for us today doing all in our power to free men everywhere from the bondage of famine, disease, ignorance, and oppression. This has to be done by political means. And it can be done only when it is free from the domination of patronage and authority. For only when those who have little are freed from our oppression will we be free of our self-righteousness and guilt. For only with them and all other men will we discover how to be human in the world today.

Dom Helder Camara, Archbishop of Olinda and Recife in Brazil, in speaking to a conference of the Catholic Churches in South America said this—and it is relevant to know where he was speaking and that he knew intimately the problem that he was discussing: "It is our task, our human and Christian duty, to help the sons of God to emerge from the sub-human situation in which they now exist." And also, in speaking of economic development, "Development therefore is the realization of man in his full human dimension, and—by the grace of God—in his divine dimension." [4] We are all too apt to be a little supercilious about the gifts of science and democracy. This is our excuse for enjoying their benefits while doing nothing for their extension among those who do not yet enjoy any of the fruits. Our misuse of science and democracy should not blind us to the truth of John Macmurray that they are the greatest gifts of Christianity to the world. If we see Jesus as Man then we have to be a little more human in our assessment of the situation and needs of others and a little more conscious of our own benefits. We need to be so committed to the finding of a human way of life for all men that it is a matter of indifference to us who gets the

[4] Dom Helder Camara, "Crisis and Response" in *Breakthrough* (April, 1969), pp. 25-26. Dom Helder Camara's speeches and addresses are to be found in full in *Church and Colonialism*, published by Sheed and Ward.

credit and a matter of joy that we work with all sorts of people of many different opinions from our own.

To believe in Jesus in human life, to see him as the revelation of Man and the key to his destiny is to step into the future and to know that the future begins today. We know that the future is upon us. The oppressions of men at the moment—their hunger, disease, and lack of hope—are no excuse for delay. Indeed they are the shocking signs of what the future must hold. They are signs because they shock us, not because they are new in the world. We must live as knowing that these things cannot be in a world of which Jesus is the light. But we have to be as certain of what must take their place. We must be committed to liberty and to men's right to liberty. We must realize that liberty means very concrete things: food and health and work. We have never to forget how Jesus spent his life. We must also realize that liberty resides in men's minds. In the world of the future which begins today men are not going to put up with authority and being told by others what to do. "Men are striving for greater truth and greater love and for the embodiment of these in personal life and human community." [5]

The only future for the world of Jesus is a world of liberty. This is certain. But the way to it is going to be very hard. But Jesus never suggested that men would find his life easy. He gave no promise that men would escape opposition, suffering, and death. There is no life without uncertainty. There is no liberty without the conflict of opinions

[5] Charles Davis, A Question of Conscience (New York: Harper, 1967), p. 196.

and the responsibility of action. There is no faith without mystery.

Jesus does not offer us the end of all our seeking. He offers us the Way, the Truth, and the Life.

To believe in Jesus is to take a leap forward into belief in God.

# Index

# Index